The Architecture of the
Italian Renaissance

1 Rome, St Peter's. The dome by Giacomo della Porta and
Domenico Fontana, 1588–90

The Architecture of the Italian Renaissance

New Revised Edition

Peter Murray

202 illustrations

Schocken Books · New York

For M.D.W. Teacher and Friend

For the second edition I have rewritten certain passages—notably those on St Peter's and on Palladio's churches—and I have taken the opportunity to incorporate many corrections suggested to me by friends and reviewers. The publishers have allowed me to add several new illustrations, and I should like to thank Mr Michael Wheeler for his help with these. The opportunity has also been taken to revise the Bibliography. For this third edition many more small changes have been made and the Bibliography has once more been extensively revised and brought up to date because there has been an enormous increase in interest in Italian architecture since 1963 when this book was first published.

It should be noted that I have consistently used the forms 1425/30 and 1425—30 to mean, first, 'at some point between 1425 and 1430', and, second, 'beginning in 1425 and ending in 1430'.

Published by arrangement with Thames & Hudson, London

Library of Congress Cataloging-in-Publication Data
Murray, Peter, 1920—
    The architecture of the Italian Renaissance.
    Reprint. Originally published: London : Thames and Hudson, 1969.
    Bibliography: p.
    Includes index.
    1. Architecture—Italy.   2. Architecture, Renaissance—Italy.   I. Title.
NA1115.M8   1986   720'.945   85-26243
ISBN 0-8052-0807-0

Manufactured in the United States of America

9 8

Contents

Introduction

Most people are overawed by the great Gothic cathedrals; the experience of walking round Canterbury or Chartres must often have given rise to the feeling that the pleasures of architecture are both real and worth cultivating. St Peter's in Rome or St Paul's in London do not have the same effect on everyone, and for this reason many people feel that Renaissance and Baroque architecture are not for them. There is a simple explanation for this difficulty in understanding, since Renaissance architecture requires knowledge on the part of the spectator as well as a readiness to accept it on its own terms. Some of the emotions aroused by a Gothic cathedral derive from the associations of the place rather than from its actual form, although the splendour of the stained-glass windows and the great soaring vaults overhead profoundly reinforce the historical and devotional associations. Renaissance architecture must be experienced as architecture, and it is only honest to say that it is no easier (and no more difficult) to understand it than it is to understand a Bach fugue. In the first place, Renaissance architecture, as its name implies, is a deliberate revival of the ideas and practices of the architects of classical antiquity and, in point of fact, it may be said that Renaissance architecture is Roman, since classical Greek architecture was almost unknown in western Europe before the eighteenth century. A Roman or Renaissance building depends for its effect upon very subtle adjustments of very simple masses, and both are based on the modular system of proportion. The module is defined as half the diameter of the column at its base and the whole of a classical building depends upon this initial proportion. Occasionally the diameter itself is used as the standard of proportion: in either case it is scale that is important, not actual dimensions. Thus, if a temple is based on a colonnade of Corinthian columns and each column is 2 feet in diameter, the module will be 1 foot, the height of the column itself will be about 18–21 feet (since a certain variation is licit), and the height of the column and capital will determine the height of the entablature, and thus of the building as a whole. Similarly, the length and width of the building will be determined by the module, since it fixes not only the size of the column but also – again within limits – the amount of space between each column. From all this it follows that every detail of a classical building is related to every other detail, and in practice the whole building is proportioned to the human body, since the column itself was thought of in antiquity as being like a human body and frequently proportionate to it in height. Together with the relationship of all the parts the classical architect sought for symmetry and harmony, so that in a blank wall pierced by three windows he would be careful to see that the height of the wall was proportioned to its width, that the openings were pierced symmetrically within it, and that the shape of the rectangle of the window bore some satisfactory relationship to the shape of the wall as a whole. From this it is evident that a little practice is needed to appreciate the multiplicity in unity of this kind of architecture, and it is also obvious that, to a sensitive eye, a moulding three inches too wide can be as distressing as a wrong note in a piece of music.

In the nineteenth century this kind of architecture lay under a deep cloud of moral disapproval. Pugin, Ruskin, and many others seemed to believe that churches in the Gothic style were Christian, whereas the classical styles were no more than an attempt to revive pagan forms. The most perfervid denunciations flowed from Ruskin: in *The Stones of Venice* he worked himself into a frenzy –

> First, let us cast out utterly whatever is connected with the Greek, Roman, or Renaissance architecture, in principle or in form. . . . It is base, unnatural, unfruitful, unenjoyable, and impious. Pagan in its origin, proud and unholy in its revival, paralysed in its old age . . an architecture invented, as it seems, to make plagiarists of its architects, slaves of its workmen, and Sybarites of its inhabitants; an architecture in which intellect is idle, invention impossible, but in which all luxury is gratified, and all insolence fortified. . . .

The foolishness of trying to look at architecture through moralistic spectacles was demonstrated by Geoffrey Scott in his classic book *The Architecture of Humanism*, first published in 1914. Unfortunately, Scott himself, while elegantly demolishing the various fallacies that prevented people from looking with unprejudiced eyes at Renaissance architecture, nevertheless fell into the trap which lurks permanently beneath the word 'humanism'. This, in the fifteenth century, meant one thing and one thing only: the study of Greek and Latin literature, both as language and as literature. It never implied any particular theological position, and indeed the humanists differed among themselves as much in this as any other group of men. The Italian humanists, however, all shared one passion, a nostalgic longing for the glory of Italy under the Romans and for the splendour of the Latin language. The artists who were associated with them naturally came to feel the same emotion for antique art that the writers felt for Latin literature; yet a moment's thought will show that neither antique art nor Roman literature is homogeneous, and the Renaissance imitations of them vary equally greatly. There is a celebrated passage in the Memorandum on Ancient Rome, presented to Pope Leo X in 1519, which describes clearly the way in which the men of the sixteenth century revered ancient Rome and yet at the same time felt themselves able to rival it:

> Therefore, O Holy Father, let it not be last in the thought of your Holiness to have a care that the little which remains of the ancient mother of glory and of the Italian name, witness of the divine spirits whose memory even today creates and moves to virtue – spirits still alive among us – should not be altogether wiped out. . . . May your Holiness, while keeping the example of the ancient world still alive among us, hasten to equal and to surpass the men of ancient times, as you even now do. . . . There are only three styles of building, which lasted from the first Emperors until the time when Rome was ruined and despoiled by the Goths and other barbarians. . . . For although in our own day architecture is active and approaches very nearly to the antique style, as may be seen in many beautiful buildings of Bramante, the ornamentation is nevertheless not made of such precious material. . . .[1]

If we compare the Palazzo Rucellai of about 1450 with the house built for himself by Giulio Romano in Mantua a hundred years later it is evident that they have little in common; and equally it is possible to compare centrally planned churches such as Brunelleschi's Sta Maria degli Angeli with Bramante's Tempietto, or churches of a more traditional Latin cross type such as Brunelleschi's Sto Spirito and Vignola's Gesù. The common factor is, of course, the adherence to the basic principles of Roman architecture, just as contemporary writers modelled themselves on Ciceronian Latin; but in both cases

[38]
[109]

9

the heritage of Christianity was bound to make an enormous difference to the outlook of the artist. In other words, Renaissance architecture has different aims, different background, and also a different constructional technique. The dome of Florence Cathedral would not have been possible without Gothic masonry techniques, yet we should never forget that one of the principal reasons for the desire to emulate the buildings of the Romans lay in their staggering and obvious superiority to the works of later ages. Even nowadays, accustomed as we are to enormous buildings and to the technical feats made possible by steel and reinforced concrete, it is still an awe-inspiring experience to stand in the Basilica of Constantine or the Pantheon. In the early fifteenth century Rome consisted of huge, stark ruins overgrown with vegetation and melancholy in their decay, while small and decrepit hovels represented the total secular building activity of a thousand years. There is a long lament by the humanist Poggio written about 1431 on the state of Rome at that time:

> This Capitoline hill, once the head and centre of the Roman Empire and the citadel of the whole world, before which every king and prince trembled, the hill ascended in triumph by so many emperors and once adorned with the gifts and spoils of so many and such great peoples, the cynosure of all the world, now lies so desolate and ruined, and so changed from its earlier condition, that vines have replaced the benches of the senators, and the Capitol has become a receptacle of dung and filth. Look at the Palatine, and there accuse Fortune, which has laid low the palace built by Nero, after the burning of the city, from the plunder of the whole world, and splendidly embellished with the assembled riches of the empire, the dwelling which, enhanced by trees, lakes, obelisks, arcades, gigantic statues, amphitheatres of vari-coloured marble, was admired by all who beheld it; all this is now so ruined that not a shadow remains that can be identified as anything but wild wasteland.[2]

The same sentiment was expressed, more tersely, by the unknown author of the epigram *Roma quanta fuit ipsa ruina docet*, which Serlio adopted as the motto of his book on the antiquities of Rome (1540). The one surviving classical author who had written on architecture, Vitruvius, was known throughout the Middle Ages, but Poggio is supposed to have rediscovered a manuscript of his treatise in the

Swiss monastery of St Gall early in the fifteenth century; and it is certainly true that from then onwards the obscure and technical Latin of Vitruvius was studied with passion, and architects began to write treatises based more or less freely on his. Vitruvius gives implicitly an account of the aims of the architect in antiquity and these aims were restated by generation after generation of architects in their own treatises. Some quotations will make quite clear what their views were on such subjects as the beauty of proportion, the harmony to be sought for in a building, and the deliberate re-creation of classical types. Vitruvius himself set the example with his definitions:

> Architecture consists of Order . . . Arrangement . . . Proportion, Symmetry, Propriety and Economy. . . .
>
> *(De Architectura*, I, ii, 1)

> The planning of temples depends on symmetry: architects must diligently understand the method of this. It arises from proportion. . . . Proportion consists in taking a fixed module, in each case, both for the parts of a building and for the whole, by which the method of symmetry is put into practice. For without symmetry and proportion no temple can have a regular plan; that is, it must have an exact proportion worked out after the fashion of the members of a well-shaped body. . . . In like fashion the members of temples ought to have dimensions of their several parts answering suitably to the general sum of their magnitude. . . . If a man lies on his back with hands and feet outspread, and the centre of a circle is located in his navel, then his hands and feet will touch the circumference: a square can also be produced in the same way . . . the height of a body from the sole of the foot to the crown of the head being equal to the span of the outstretched arms.
>
> *(De Arch.,* III, i, 1–3)

> I shall define Beauty to be a harmony of all the parts, in whatsoever subject it appears, fitted together with such proportion and connection, that nothing could be added, diminished or altered but for the worse. . . .   (Alberti, *De re aedificatoria*, VI, 2)

> The windows in the Temple ought to be small and high, so that nothing but the sky may be seen through them; to the intent that both the priests that are employed in the performance of Divine offices, and those that assist upon account of devotion, may not

11

have their minds in any way diverted. . . . For this reason the Ancients were very often contented without any other aperture beside the doorway. (Alberti, *De re aed.*, VII, 12)

As Vitruvius says, there are three things to be considered in any building, without which no edifice is worthy of praise: utility or commodity; durability; and beauty. . . . Beauty will be the result of a beautiful form and from the correspondence between the whole and its parts, and of the parts between themselves as well as to the whole; thus, buildings may appear as a single, well-finished, body within which all the members agree, and all members are necessary for what is desired. . . . (Palladio, *I Quattro Libri*, I, 1)

Temples may be round, quadrangular, of six, eight, or more sides, all of which tend towards the circle; cruciform, and in many other shapes and figures according to the different intentions of men. . . . But the most beautiful and most regular forms, from which the others derive, are the circle and quadrangle; and therefore Vitruvius speaks only of these two. . . .

Thus we read that the men of Antiquity, in building their temples, set themselves to observe Decorum, which is one of the most beautiful constituents of Architecture. And we, who know not false Gods, in order to observe Decorum in the form of temples, will choose the most perfect and excellent, which is the circle; for it alone is simple, uniform, equal, strong, and adapted to its purpose. Thus, we should make our Temples circular . . . most apt to demonstrate the Unity, the infinite Essence, the Uniformity and Justice of GOD. . . .[3]

Those churches are also to be praised which are in the form of a Cross . . . for they represent to the eye of the beholder that Wood, from which our salvation hung. It was of this shape that I made the Church of S. Giorgio Maggiore in Venice. . . .

Of all the colours none is more suited to Temples than white, for the purity of this colour, as of life, is most pleasing to GOD. But if they are to be painted then there should not be any pictures of a kind to prevent the mind from contemplation of Divine things; for Temples should never depart from gravity or from those things which, when we see them, inflame our souls with worship and the desire of good works.

(Palladio, *I Quattro Libri*, IV, 2)

Classical buildings of a secular type were obviously easier to revive than were the pagan temples of antiquity, unsuited as they were to the Christian liturgy, and especially so in their associations. Thus, for example, the classical *insula* or block of flats develops organically into the Italian palace, and the fascinating spectacle of the past growing into the present is more clearly to be seen in Italy than anywhere else in the world. Almost the same thing is true of the forms of churches, as distinct from temples. In fact, the Renaissance architects hardly thought of themselves as reviving Roman forms since the main types of Christian church had been laid down in the early fourth century under the Emperor Constantine, and for.the fifteenth and sixteenth centuries the Christian Roman Empire in the century between the Edict of Milan in 313 and the Sack of Rome by the Vandals in 410 was one of the high points of classical art. For this reason it could never have occurred to Brunelleschi or Bramante to think of a centrally planned church as 'un-Christian' and, indeed, their view was that Gothic architecture was the architecture of barbarians. The importation of Gothic ideas into Italy was slow and late; that it happened at all is due to historical circumstances, and in one sense at least the men of the Renaissance felt that they were returning to the aims and ideals of their forefathers when they tried to clear away the wreckage of the barbarian centuries and find their way back into the broad, straight, stream of 'the good manner of building'.

The great French scholar Emile Mâle expressed this perfectly in two sentences:

> Thus, the traveller who made his way from the Colosseum to St Peter's by way of Constantine's Basilica and the Pantheon, who visited the Sistine Chapel and the best of Raphael's Stanze, has seen, in a day, the finest things in Rome. He will have learnt, at the same time, what the Renaissance was: it was Antiquity ennobled by the Christian faith.[4]

2 Florence, S. Miniato. Façade, *c.* 1090

CHAPTER ONE

Romanesque and Gothic in Tuscany

Italian architecture does not begin with the year 1300; but this book begins in the thirteenth century because it must begin somewhere, and also because of the nature of Italian Gothic. For many years Italian Gothic architecture has been rather out of fashion. This is no doubt mainly due to Ruskin's intemperate advocacy of Venetian Gothic which was to result in so many railway stations and town halls, erected in an unsuitable climate, and now dank and grimy. In fact, Italian Gothic architecture is different from French, English, or German Gothic but not necessarily inferior. The causes which underlie the forms used by Italian architects of the thirteenth and fourteenth centuries are to be found in the history and the climate of Italy, but it is necessary to point out that at this period Italy itself was an abstraction. The present Italian State is a creation of the late nineteenth century, and during the whole of the Renaissance Italy consisted of a large number of small and very highly individualistic independent powers. The great powers were Venice, Florence, Naples, Milan, and the Papal States centred on Rome, but this fragmentation is the principal reason for the great differences between Venetian and Florentine art; differences at least as great as those between English and French art in the same period.

The first and far the most important factor in the development of all the arts in the whole of Italy was the heritage of classical antiquity. This is particularly to be seen in places like Rome or Verona where a great number of buildings still survive from Roman times. It is also true, in a rather more indefinable way, of places like Florence where republican sentiment was very consciously modelled on the Roman Republic, so that a tendency to regard the classical past as a norm of civilized behaviour as well as of architecture is very strongly to be felt. This undying classical tradition is, of course, a fundamental characteristic of all Italian art. Two other factors began to operate in the thirteenth century, and it was the combination of these with the classical tradition which gave rise to Italian Gothic architecture.

The first was the phenomenal expansion of the new religious Orders; the Orders founded in the early thirteenth century by St Francis and St Dominic. Both expanded so fast that by the end of the century their members were to be numbered in thousands. These Orders differed very markedly from the older monastic Orders in that their members did not live shut away in monasteries but spent much of their time in preaching, and both Orders were characteristic of the new and more human approach to religion which is one of the essential characteristics of the thirteenth century. Because of their enormous popularity it was very soon evident that many new churches were going to be needed and, which is more important, a new kind of church, primarily designed to hold very large congregations all of whom would have to be able to hear the preacher or to see the religious dramas which were often presented there.

At the moment when these new churches were being built the other factor came into operation. This was the moment of the greatest flowering of Gothic architecture in the north, and particularly in France, so that modern architecture in the thirteenth century meant French Gothic architecture and the great feats of construction of the French architects provided a model for the rest of the world. The direct influence of French architecture can be seen most clearly in Milan Cathedral, begun in 1386 and worked on by French and German architects as well as local masons. Nevertheless, Milan Cathedral remains unique in Italy, nor is it really very like a French building. To a certain extent French Gothic forms were imposed from without, because the Cistercian Order had the curious characteristic that all its monasteries, whether in the wilds of Yorkshire or in the south of Italy, deliberately imitated the form of the mother-house at Cîteaux near Dijon. The Abbey of Chiaravalle near Milan was founded in 1135 and is thus a very early example of this French type on Italian soil.

It was inevitable that these foreign ideas should come into collision with the existing Italian Romanesque style. The church of S. Miniato [2] just outside Florence has a façade which can be dated about 1090. The characteristic form of this façade is distantly reminiscent of antique architecture, with its round arches carried on columns and its triangular pediment. The colouristic effect obtained by the contrast between off-white marble and the dark greenish, almost black, marble used to emphasize the architectural members is a feature of this

16

Romanesque style which does not appear to have a parallel in antiquity. Nevertheless, it seems that in the thirteenth and fourteenth centuries these buildings were commonly believed to be very much older than was actually the case; for example, we know that the Baptistry in Florence was generally held to be an antique pagan temple converted to Christian use. It is probably safe, therefore, to assume that the traditionalists thought of a building like S. Miniato or the Baptistry as actual survivals from the Roman past and therefore better models for imitation than new-fangled French ideas. [13]

An example of the style which arose from this conflict is conveniently provided by the great church at Assisi which was begun immediately after the canonization of St Francis in 1228. The Upper Church (there are two churches one above the other), which was consecrated in 1253, consists of a single, very large nave with no aisles at the sides. This immense open space is covered by a stone-vaulted roof, the weight of which is carried on ribs which in turn are supported by columns. By comparison with any French Gothic building of equal importance the columns are very short and the spaces between them very wide. At the same time, the fact that there are no aisles means that S. Francesco at Assisi is a wide, open, single space where its French counterpart is immensely high and is divided up by the aisles into a sequence of spaces with all the emphasis on verticality. [3]

The hotter climate of Central Italy produces yet another difference, for any of the greater northern Gothic cathedrals impress us by their extreme height and by the fact that all the supports are concentrated into a few very slender columns with enormous windows set between them. Such windows would obviously be impractical in Assisi, which means that there are large spaces of empty wall between each of the load-bearing columns. These spaces were naturally used for decoration with paintings, and the famous cycle of twenty-eight scenes from the life of St Francis which decorates the Upper Church of Assisi not only makes the best possible use of the wall space available, but also adds very markedly to the general impression of horizontality which is so un-French and indeed so un-Gothic a characteristic.

Fundamentally, therefore, the difference between French and Italian Gothic architecture comes down to the question of the shape of each bay; that is to say, the relationship between the width, length, and height of the spaces covered by a single ribbed vault and bounded

3 Assisi, S. Francesco, the Upper Church, consecrated 1253

on plan by the bases of the four supporting columns. The typical French bay is very wide in relation to the space between the columns on the long axis, whereas the bays at Assisi are much squarer in form.

The square bay tends to be rather characteristic of Italian Gothic architecture and the evolution of this type of design can be studied in the earliest Cistercian churches in Italy, notably in two south of Rome at Casamari and Fossanova, both of which were completed [4] early in the thirteenth century. Fossanova follows the pattern established in the great church at Cîteaux very closely. The general type is that of a Latin cross with a square-ended choir, small square chapels at the sides, and a square crossing, but with a long nave consisting of rectangular bays, considerably wider than they are long, linked to bays in the aisles which are almost square. The nave at Fossanova [8] dates from 1187 and the church was consecrated in 1208. It is, therefore, slightly earlier than one of the great French Gothic cathedrals such as Rheims. Both Rheims and Fossanova have high stone vaults carried on slender columns with half-columns attached to the arcade wall, but the great difference between them consists in the architect's approach to the basic problem of supporting the weight of the great stone vault. The French Gothic system was a superb piece of engineering in which the weight of the roof was carried partly as a direct vertical thrust on the slender piers, and partly as an outward thrust carried on one or even two rows of flying buttresses. These buttresses took the thrust which could not be carried on the columns and diverted it downwards over the aisle roof. The very large and elaborate pinnacles which can usually be seen on any big Gothic church are, in effect, counter-weights which divert the thrust of the vault vertically downwards and the decorative quality which they impart to the silhouette of the church should not conceal from us their essentially structural function. Nevertheless, no Italian architect would have wished to break the simplicity of the outside line of his church by spiky pinnacles, and the sober classicism which the Italians sought in the exterior of their churches could be maintained, therefore, only by forgoing the structural advantages of the flying-buttress system. This, in turn, means that the weight of the vault must be carried entirely on the internal columns and on the outside walls. At Fossanova there are buttresses set against the walls but they are small and more like classical pilasters than any form of flying buttress. The inside of the church, therefore, necessarily has a

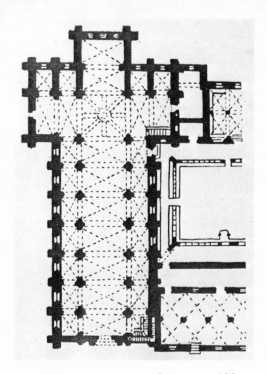 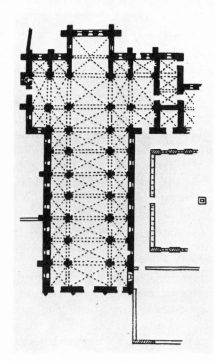

ITALIAN GOTHIC
CHURCH PLANS

4 Fossanova Abbey.
Consecrated 1208

5 S. Galgano, near Siena,
c. 1218

totally different appearance from that of a French Gothic church and both inside and outside are entirely lacking in that feeling of forces maintained in equilibrium which gives such an exhilarating quality to the best northern architecture.

[5]

[6, 9, 28]

This modified Cistercian Gothic architecture was introduced into Tuscany about 1218 in the church of S. Galgano, near Siena. S. Galgano, which is now a ruin, seems to have been designed by an architect who had worked at Casamari and it follows the established Cistercian pattern very closely. Its importance lies in the fact that it introduced these ideas into Tuscany, where the first really important and independent church in a truly Italian style was begun in Florence about 1246. This was the very large church of Sta Maria Novella, built for the Dominican Order and partially subsidized by the Florentine State. The exact dates of the various parts of the church are still controversial but it certainly took a very long time to build since it was begun about 1246, the nave was not begun until 1279,

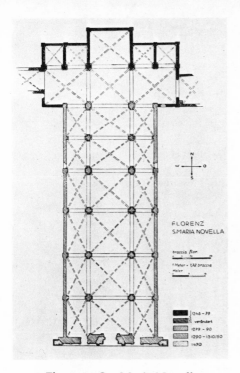

FLORENZ
S.MARIA NOVELLA

braccia fior.

1 Meter = 1,72 braccia
Meter

1246-79
verändert
1279-90
1290-1310/50
1470

6 Florence, Sta Maria Novella.
Begun 1246

7 Florence, Sta Croce.
Begun 1294/5

and the façade, begun in 1310, was not finished until 1470. Nevertheless, the interior and the plan make it the most important church of its date. It was begun as a new foundation for the Order of Preachers and it was therefore conditioned by the need to house a very large congregation in the nave and to provide the best possible acoustics. Unlike monastic churches, it was not necessary to provide a large choir, but a number of smaller chapels under the patronage of private families were very soon added.

The choice of a stone vault instead of an open timbered roof – the common Tuscan form at this period – was probably partly for grandeur of effect, partly because it had come in as the new French fashion, and partly also because of its superior acoustic qualities. The interior of the church is open, spacious, and rather horizontal in feeling. The main element of design is a square nave bay with aisles on either side which are much longer than they are wide and are approximately half the width of the central square. This is quite

8 Fossanova Abbey. The nave, 1187

different from the tunnel-like effect of Fossanova or S. Galgano,
where it is the aisle bays which are square and the nave bays are about
twice as wide as they are long, thus making the columns come very
much closer together and giving automatically a tunnel-like effect
with great emphasis on the vertical lines of the columns and the ribs
of the vaults. The open spaciousness of Sta Maria Novella is obviously
very much better from the purely practical point of view of accom-
modating a congregation which can both see and hear the preacher.
The differences between Fossanova and Sta Maria Novella do not,

9 Florence, Sta Maria Novella. The nave, begun 1279

however, end with the difference in plan. The extreme verticality of
Fossanova is due also to the fact that the height of the arcade is very
much less than that of the clerestory, whereas the heights in Sta Maria
Novella are approximately equal, thus bringing the line of the roof
visually nearer the ground. There are many other small points of
difference, but two are particularly relevant. They are the types of
capital and half-column which carry the arcade arches in Sta Maria
Novella, and the colouristic effect of the use of dark grey *pietra serena*
set against the white plaster walls. The columns and capitals are much

23

nearer to classical ones than are their counterparts at Fossanova and the use of the black and white membering was an established Romanesque technique in Tuscany.

In other words, Sta Maria Novella represents a compromise between French Gothic structural principles and the equilibrium and harmony of the Italian classical heritage. This new compromise abandons the basic Gothic striving after towering height, just as it rejects the supremely skilful engineering systems of the French cathedrals. Nevertheless, the new Tuscan Gothic style has a number of important buildings to its credit, and it lasted for nearly two hundred years. There was a great deal of building activity following the reform of the Florentine Constitution in 1250, and it was partly occasioned by the need for new churches. In Florence itself the church of Sta Croce and the Cathedral are two of the most important successors to Sta Maria Novella. The church of Sta Maria sopra Minerva in Rome is almost a direct copy of Sta Maria Novella and was also built for the Dominican Order. It has the distinction of being the only pure Gothic church in Rome before the nineteenth century.

The problem of authorship of the greater Tuscan Gothic churches is rather involved. We have no certain knowledge of the architects of Sta Maria Novella, though it was traditionally designed by two Dominican friars. On the other hand, the famous sculptor, Nicola Pisano, is mentioned as the architect of at least one Florentine church – SS. Trinità – which he is supposed to have built in the 1250s. The attribution may well be correct, but its importance lies principally in the fact that Nicola Pisano trained two of the major artists of the next generation, both of whom were architects as well as sculptors. They were his own son, Giovanni Pisano, and Arnolfo di Cambio, and, because we have very little definite information about the architectural style of either of these men, we have to make as much as possible of what we can deduce from the style of Nicola Pisano and to relate it to the work of both Giovanni and Arnolfo. Giovanni Pisano designed the façade of the Cathedral at Siena and seems on the whole to have continued his father's style with a strong dash of French influence, although this is much more perceptible in his sculpture than in his architecture.

Arnolfo appears for the first time as an architect in the year 1300 when he is recorded as working on Florence Cathedral and as a

10 Florence, Sta Croce. The nave, begun 1294/5

famous builder of churches. He was apparently so famous that he was exempt from taxation but, unfortunately, he died quite soon after this (between 1302 and 1310) and Florence Cathedral has been very much altered since 1300. Indeed, the main façade is barely one hundred years old and it is difficult to be certain how much of the existing church is by him. Two other important buildings in Florence are attributed to him although there is no documentary evidence in support of the ascriptions. They are the abbey church known as the Badia and the much more important church of Sta Croce. The Badia was built between 1284 and 1310, but was altered in the seventeenth century. It has certain points in common with SS. Trinità, so that if the Badia is by Arnolfo and if SS. Trinità is by Nicola Pisano, the master–pupil relationship can be seen in the two buildings.

[7, 10]   The church of Sta Croce is more important because it is a much larger and more ambitious building. It is the main church in Florence of the Order of St Francis and was therefore built in deliberate rivalry with the Dominican Sta Maria Novella. The Franciscans themselves were bitterly divided since some of them wished to observe the original rule of absolute poverty and others clearly wished to emulate the Dominicans, who were not so bound. In point of fact, the Franciscans attracted very large charitable donations, largely from the great merchant banking families who had good reason to feel tender in their consciences on the subject of usury – hence the large number of family chapels in many of these friars' churches. The present building was begun in 1294 or 1295 but was exceptionally slow in construction, and consecration was delayed until 1442, largely because of the opposition of the stricter Franciscans, known as Observantists. Like the Cathedral, the present façade is entirely nineteenth century. We know that the nave was still unfinished in 1375, long after Arnolfo had died, but it is likely that he made a wooden model and that this was followed. The interior shows a disposition rather different from that of Sta Maria Novella. The two main features are the open timber roof and the different relationship between the nave and aisle bays. The open roof, much lighter than stone vaulting, means that the columns supporting the whole can be very light and something of the same effect of airiness as that in Sta Maria Novella is maintained in the interior. On the other hand, the plan shows that neither the aisle nor the nave is square. The aisle bays are long, and the nave bays are nearly twice as wide as they are long; that is to say, the architect

26

seems to have reverted to the Cistercian type of bay. The horizontal emphasis is, however, very marked, so that there is no likelihood of confusing Sta Croce with any non-Florentine church.

Both the Badia and Sta Croce are attributed to Arnolfo on stylistic grounds but it is certainly true that both have features which can be found, even if somewhat modified, in the Cathedral; and it is therefore possible to assert that the basic plan of the Cathedral is by Arnolfo.   [11] The Cathedral was begun in 1294 and the document which mentions Arnolfo is of 1300, so he was presumably in charge from the beginning. The church itself was intended to be as large and impressive as possible and the expense was underwritten by the Florentine Republic. Pisa and Siena, the two most important rivals of Florence, both had large, domed, Cathedrals and it is evident that Florence Cathedral was always intended to be stone vaulted and to have a very large dome indeed, simply to outdo the Pisans and the Sienese. A little later, the Sienese attempted to rebuild their Cathedral on a colossal scale, so vast that the existing Cathedral, which is quite large, would have been no more than one transept of the proposed building. This project, which must always have seemed optimistic, was brought to a complete standstill by the ravages of the Black Death in 1348, from which Siena never really recovered. The Florentines almost over-reached themselves in their desire for an impressive church since the problem of the dome was to remain unsolved for about a century and a quarter before the genius of Brunelleschi was to find a solution to the apparently impossible problem of covering it.

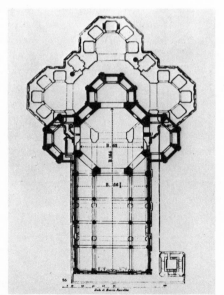

11 Florence, Cathedral.
Begun 1294. Plans by Arnolfo
and Francesco Talenti

[11]   The plan of Florence Cathedral was considerably modified by Francesco Talenti, who became Capomaestro (architect-in-chief) in 1351, but it is now generally agreed that the smaller of the two plans on page 27 represents Arnolfo's original project which Talenti enlarged but did not essentially vary. Arnolfo also built a small part of the original façade and part of the side walls as well as planning a dome over the crossing. The painter Giotto, who was appointed Capomaestro in 1334 simply because he was the most famous Florentine artist of the day, had no architectural knowledge and confined himself to designing the separate Campanile which stands like a tower beside the façade. In fact, however, Giotto's Campanile is not entirely as he designed it and the entire Cathedral was subjected to a series of modifications throughout the whole of the fourteenth century. The façade was much altered by Talenti and numerous schemes for rebuilding it were begun and abandoned at various dates until finally, between 1876 and 1886, the present Neo-Gothic façade was designed and built by Emilio De Fabris. It is clear, however, from the surviving fragments of Arnolfo's original coloured marble decoration on the side walls that the present facade is in some respects not too far from the original designer's intention.

The plan in its present form consists of four very large bays with aisles half the width of the nave bays, which are themselves wider than square and very similar to the Sta Croce type (compare plates 7 and 11). The principal difference between the two churches lies in the fact that the Cathedral has a stone vault which must therefore be carried on very solid piers, whereas the wooden roof of Sta Croce

[12, 10] does not demand such massive supports. At the east end the churches differ considerably, for the Cathedral expands into an octagon on three sides of which there are great tribunes of triconch shape. Thus, the total effect of the interior is that of a centrally planned octagonal building with spaces opening out from the octagon, and the nave is only one among others. The interior can be compared with that of Sta Croce or Sta Maria Novella and its open spaciousness, classical pilaster forms, and emphatically horizontal string-course combine to create an effect totally unlike the French Gothic cathedrals which were its distant ancestors, so that it can now be seen as the culmination of a specifically Tuscan building tradition. Furthermore, the Romanesque style in Tuscany can clearly be seen on the outside, both in the use of coloured marble inlays and in the choice of the domed octagon

28

12 Florence, Cathedral. The nave

[13] at the crossing which is clearly related to the Baptistry which stands only a few yards away. The Baptistry of Florence is very difficult to date with any precision (it is perhaps of the eighth century) but we know, from contemporary sources, that in the fourteenth century it was traditionally regarded as a temple of Mars which had been adapted for Christian usage.

The dome projected by Arnolfo may, or may not, have had a drum and it is by no means clear whether either Arnolfo or Talenti ever gave serious thought to the problem of spanning the enormous opening. By the end of the fourteenth century it became evident that something would have to be done one day and rather reluctantly a number of architects tried to devise a means of covering an opening 140 feet across. We know from the frescoes in the Spanish Chapel in Sta Maria Novella that at least one unofficial project was made about 1367, showing a slightly pointed dome without a drum, but nothing was really done until the problem became urgent, early in the fifteenth century.

This chapter has been concerned with Italian Gothic in its relationship to the style which was to develop out of it: the splendid achievements of the Gothic architects in Venice and Lombardy have been neglected, simply because they have almost no relevance to the history of Renaissance architecture.

13 Florence, Cathedral and Baptistry

CHAPTER TWO

Brunelleschi

Filippo Brunelleschi was born in 1377 and died in 1446. Like many other great artists of the early fifteenth century, he was trained originally as a goldsmith and entered the Goldsmiths' Guild in Florence in 1404. Before then he had already started to work as a sculptor, since he took part in the competition, held in 1401, for the commission for the new doors for the Baptistry. It was won by Ghiberti, and we are told that Brunelleschi went to Rome with the sculptor Donatello as soon as he knew that he had lost the competition. This is quite likely. Certainly Brunelleschi and Donatello were close friends, and, with the painter Masaccio, the three men were the representatives of the most advanced painting, sculpture, and architecture of the day. It is of considerable importance that Brunelleschi visited Rome on several occasions, for there can be no doubt that it was his close study of the constructional principles of the surviving Roman ruins that enabled him to devise a means of covering the area of the dome of the Cathedral, an achievement which has made his name immortal in Florence.

Brunelleschi is usually credited with the creation of 'the Renaissance style' in architecture, but this is subject to a number of reservations. It is, however, certain that he was the first man to begin to comprehend the structural system of classical architecture and to adapt its principles to modern needs. Perhaps the most important thing about his dome is the fact that it is a feat of engineering which could not have been carried out by anyone else in the fifteenth century. It is not, however, a piece of classicism in the archaeological sense, or in the sense in which Alberti was to understand Roman architecture only a few years later.

Brunelleschi was first consulted on the Cathedral of Florence as early as 1404, but this was on a routine matter. Nevertheless, by this time it was evident that an attempt would have to be made to cover the crossing of the Cathedral and there can be no doubt that the Florentines themselves were anxious to demonstrate their cultural superiority by erecting a dome $138\frac{1}{2}$ feet across, while at the same

time they were well aware of the difficulties inherent in the undertaking and the ridicule which would be heaped upon them by the
Pisans, the Sienese, the Lucchesi and, indeed, the inhabitants of every
town for many miles around if the attempt were made and failed.
The reason for this anxiety is the simple fact that all arches – and a
dome is no more than an arch rotated on its axis – are built on a
wooden framework called 'centering'. A horizontal wooden beam
is laid across an opening in a wall at the point at which the arch begins
to spring. A wooden framework, either semicircular or pointed, is
erected on this cross-beam and the framework supports the bricks or
stones composing the arch until the stone in the centre (the keystone)
is placed in position. The keystone is wedge-shaped so that once the
arch is built the centering can be removed and all the stones will press
one against the other in such a way that the arch remains stable;
mortar between the stones is not essential, since the wedges are really
held in place by the force of gravity. From this it is obvious that an
arch is limited in size only by the size and strength of the timber
available for centering.

Since the octagonal opening of the drum of Florence Cathedral,
which was ready by 1412 or 1413, was nearly 140 feet across and
about 180 feet above the ground, it was impossible to build a wooden
framework strong enough to support a dome. Indeed, no trees could
be found big enough to bridge the gap and even if they had, the
weight of the timber would have broken the centering long before
any stone was put on it. This is probably the reason why each succes-
sive capomaestro concentrated his attention on any part of the
Cathedral rather than the dome. As late as the sixteenth century it is
clear that an aura of mystery still surrounded Brunelleschi's feat.
Vasari, in his life of Brunelleschi, written about 1550, tells us that the
suggestion was seriously advanced that the whole of the tribune
should be filled with earth and that on top of this the dome should be
built. It was then proposed that all the earth should be disposed of by
the expedient of mixing pennies in at intervals so that all the Florentine
children would come and take the earth away in order to get at the
money.

In 1418 the Operai (overseers of the works) announced a public
competition, but we know that Brunelleschi was already working on
a model, presumably made of stone. In 1417 he had already been paid
for drawings, and a wooden model had been made. Ghiberti, who

[14]

had defeated Brunelleschi in the Baptistry Doors competition, was also called in and submitted a model. In 1420 both Brunelleschi and Ghiberti were appointed, together with a mason, to act as supervisors and to build the dome.

The construction of the dome began on 7 August 1420, and was finished as far as the base of the lantern on 1 August 1436. Before work began Brunelleschi had already built two smaller domes, more or less as trial runs; and, although these have not survived intact, we do know that they were very small, hemispherical in shape, and constructed on ribs. It is also clear that Ghiberti and Brunelleschi did not get on at all well together, and there are later stories of how Brunelleschi pretended to be ill at critical moments so as to expose Ghiberti's incompetence. Ghiberti, on the other hand, in his auto-biography, declares that he worked on the dome for eighteen years and implicitly claims half the credit. It seems very likely that Ghiberti's part in the early stages of the dome was greater than later generations gave him credit for, but it is also certain that from about 1420 onwards the actual construction and indeed the invention of new machinery was Brunelleschi's work alone. A document of 1423 refers to him as 'inventor and governor' and we know that Ghiberti was dismissed in 1425 just at the moment when the construction was becoming very difficult. It should, however, be remembered that in 1425 Ghiberti had been given the important commission for the second Baptistry Doors, and no doubt he had to give his time entirely to them.

When construction began the two major problems which had to be faced were that no centering of the traditional type was possible, and, to make matters worse, the drum over the octagon already existed. This drum has no external abutments, so that any weight resting on it must exert the absolute minimum of side thrust. In a Gothic building this would hardly matter since the side thrusts would have been provided for by flying buttresses at the angles of the octagon. This was impossible in Florence, where flying buttresses would have been visually unacceptable, and in any case there was nowhere to put them. This is the structural reason which conditions the pointed shape of the dome. Brunelleschi, like every other classically-minded architect, would have wished to build a hemi-spherical dome because of its perfection of shape and because the great Roman domes, above all the Pantheon, are hemispherical. Because of the problem of abutments, a pointed dome had to be adopted, since the side thrusts from a pointed dome are very much less than those exerted by a ribbed hemisphere. A dome like the Pantheon, which is solid concrete, exerts no side thrusts at all, but, on the other hand, the dead weight of such a dome would have crushed the existing drum. There was, therefore, only one solution, which was to build a dome pointed in section and supported on ribs with the lightest possible infilling between them. Brunelleschi's solution, from any point of view, was a work of genius. The axonometric drawing[5] shows how the work was done. There are eight major ribs springing from the angles of the octagon and sixteen minor ribs set in pairs between each pair of major ribs (this idea almost certainly came from the Baptistry, which is a domed octagon with eight and sixteen ribs). The skeleton is completed by horizontal arches which tie the major and the minor ribs together and absorb the side thrusts. There are two shells to the dome, an outer skin and an inner one, intended, in Brunelleschi's own words, to keep out the damp and to give greater magnificence. This is the first known use of a double shell dome and it is obviously one of the ways in which the weight was considerably reduced. The eight major ribs are clearly visible from the outside, while the minor ones can be seen only from inside the two shells, where there is also a passage leading to the base of the lantern.

[15]

By 1425 construction had reached about one-third of the way up, to the point where the curve was beginning to move sharply inwards and it was at this point that the lack of centering posed the greatest problems. Brunelleschi, who had presented a long memorandum to the building committee before he began to build, had left himself a free hand by pointing out in advance that in an undertaking of this kind practice alone would show what was necessary. In the event, he made only one major change, and that was the substitution of brick for stone in the upper parts, since this was lighter. For the rest, his unfailingly fertile imagination produced a whole series of new mechanical devices, such as cranes and machines for handling the stone blocks; and it is also said that he arranged for a complete canteen high above ground level, in order to save the men wasting time going down for their meals.

The solution to the apparently insoluble problem of the centering was to build the dome in horizontal courses, each of which was bonded to its predecessor in such a way that each course carried its own weight and was strong enough to support the work on the next

34

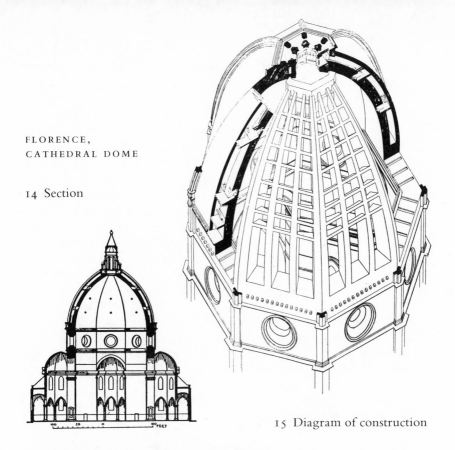

FLORENCE,
CATHEDRAL DOME

14 Section

15 Diagram of construction

one until the ring had been closed, and, by being closed, it became able to support the next course. A certain herring-bone pattern in the masonry courses has also been observed and there can be no doubt that Brunelleschi learnt this from the study he had made during his various stays in Rome of ancient Roman construction. There is a much later drawing in the Uffizi in Florence showing a dome with herring-bone courses and annotated 'how they build domes in Florence without centering'. Once again, it would seem that for a thousand years no one had really understood or had even attempted to understand how the enormous Roman vaults and domes had been put up, and Brunelleschi must have worked the whole thing out by wandering among the ruins and asking himself questions which no one else at that time had even thought of formulating.

When the dome proper was completed there was a large ring about 20 feet in diameter where the ribs converged to an open eye. It is a curious fact that although it was necessary to keep the dome as light as possible, yet the forces acting on this eye were such that the ribs themselves tended to sit back on their haunches and therefore to burst the ring open. In order to meet this problem, the lantern had to act as a sort of stopper and had therefore to be relatively heavy. This explains the size and elaboration of the lantern as it exists. A competition was held in 1436 which, not surprisingly, was won by Brunelleschi. We know that he made a complete model of his design and it is highly likely that this is the model which still exists in the Cathedral Museum. Work was not begun on the actual construction until 1446, a few months before Brunelleschi's death, but the execution was entrusted to his friend and follower, Michelozzo, and the existing building follows Brunelleschi's design in every respect. The Gothic ribs of the dome are very skilfully linked by a kind of flying buttress which supports the core of the lantern, and, by means of inverted classical consoles, links the ribs to the octagon turret. The general appearance is, as one might expect, as classical as possible, and the

16 Florence,
Spedale degli
Innocenti. Façade,
1419–24

lantern of the Baptistry just across the street provided the prototype. [13] As a final decorative touch, Brunelleschi also built the exedrae at the base of the drum between 1439 and 1445. These reflect the change in his style which can be dated to the 1430s and it is to his other works that one must turn in order to get a clearer picture of the evolution of his style when it was not conditioned, as it inevitably was in the Cathedral, by existing problems of construction and design. There can be no doubt that the lingering Gothic spirit of the dome of the Cathedral was not desired by Brunelleschi, but was accepted by him because no feasible alternative solution to the problems of statics presented itself.

The first expression of Brunelleschi's own architectural principles, or, to put it another way, the first truly Renaissance work, was the Foundling Hospital – the Spedale degli Innocenti – built between [16] 1419 and 1424. This, which was the first hospital for foundling children in the world, was built at the expense of Brunelleschi's own Guild, that of the Silk Merchants and Goldsmiths. From the point of view of architecture the important part of this building is the outside

loggia, since the hospital itself was completed by Brunelleschi's followers when he himself, in 1425, was far too busy with the dome of the Cathedral to attend to anything else. There is a prototype for such a hospital building with a vaulted loggia outside it in the hospital at Lastra a Signa near Florence, built in 1411, and at first glance there is little to choose between the two. It is, however, when one looks more closely at the arches, the vaults, and the details of the Foundling Hospital that one sees how the Early Renaissance style is both deeply rooted in the Tuscan Romanesque and yet at the same time presents a number of new elements derived from classical antiquity. The loggia consists of a series of round arches, with a horizontal element above them, and a vault, consisting of small domes carried on the columns of the loggia and on corbels on the surface of the hospital wall. The domed bays are square in plan, not cross vaulted but of the simple classic shape. The profile – the inner face – of the arches is flat and not triangular in section as a Gothic arch would be. This is because the arches are archivolts; that is, they are the entablatures of classical antiquity bent upwards to form semicircular arches. Similarly, the columns, the capitals, and the corbels are all of classic type, while the columns have dosserets inserted between the capitals and the base of the vaults. Dosserets are more Byzantine than Roman, but they occur in Tuscan Romanesque churches such as SS. Apostoli in Florence. It is highly likely that at this stage of his career Brunelleschi thought that the tenth century SS. Apostoli was an Early Christian (i.e. fourth or fifth century) building, for it was not until much later that he began to distinguish between the purer forms of classical antiquity and those of the later centuries. This use of non–classical models can be proved from a curious circumstance in the Foundling Hospital. Above the round arches there runs a long entablature supported at the ends by large pilasters; this, however, departs radically from classical precedent at the extreme ends of the building, where the architrave suddenly bends downwards. This is a feature which occurs, in the Baptistry at Florence. It is clear, therefore, that the Baptistry, the date of which has been put by modern historians anywhere in the millennium between the fourth and the fourteenth centuries, was for Brunelleschi, at that stage in his development, an architectural exemplar of the same validity as the great Roman ruins. The arcading and the tabernacle windows also derive from the Baptistry.

38

Some reflections of Brunelleschi's architectural innovations can be seen in the work of his friends Masaccio and Donatello. Masaccio's fresco of the Holy Trinity was probably painted before November 1425, and the niche by Donatello and Michelozzo on the church of Orsanmichele was built between 1422 and 1425: both are more truly classical in feeling than the Loggia degli Innocenti, but neither could have existed without it.

Brunelleschi built two large basilical churches in Florence, both completed after his death but showing the development of his style in his later years, and both of them became patterns of the Latin cross type of plan. The earlier of the two is S. Lorenzo, the parish church of [19, 20] the Medici family. This was begun in 1419, when a plan was drawn up for rebuilding a much older church on the site. Many chapels were necessary since it was a monastic foundation, and Brunelleschi therefore adapted the type which had been established in the last years of the thirteenth century at Sta Croce. The basic shape is a large Latin cross with a square central crossing, a square choir and smaller square chapels at either side of it. The architectural weakness of this type of plan can be seen by comparing Sta Croce with S. Lorenzo. In the [7, 20] earlier church there is a strongly accented directional feeling from the west towards the east end, but the three great axes of nave and aisles rather peter out in a clutter of small chapels at the east end which do not bear any clearly established proportional relationship to the nave. Since the number of monks living in the house determined the number of chapels necessary, it was often unavoidable that they should be small. In S. Lorenzo Brunelleschi met this difficulty by extending the chapels round the transepts in such a way that he obtained the same number (ten in all) at the east end, but each individual chapel is now related in proportion both to the choir and to the nave and aisles. It was for this reason that his two Florentine churches became examples of proportional planning, since they took an established type and subjected it to a mathematical discipline. The basic unit is the square of the crossing. This square is repeated exactly to form both transepts and choir, and the nave is then made four squares long. The aisle bays are rectangular and exactly half the width of the main square bay. In this way, the spectator standing in one of the aisles looks across the transept to the opening of a chapel which is related in size to the nave and aisles; and the total effect is therefore much more harmonious than was the case in a church like Sta Croce.

[17, 18]

In order to find space for ten chapels of this larger size, it was necessary to extend them round the ends and both sides of the transept, which in turn left an awkward gap at the angles. This angle was satisfactorily filled by using the space for two sacristies, known as the Old and New Sacristies. The new one was allowed for in Brunelleschi's plan but was not built for more than a hundred years. The Old Sacristy was begun in 1419, when the plan for rebuilding the church was first established, and, because it was paid for by a member of the Medici family, it was built quite rapidly between August 1421 (when the foundation-stone was laid) and 1428. The sculptural decoration by Donatello is generally thought to be rather later, perhaps of the mid 1430s. Since the sacristy was finished before the rest of the church, it may be considered as a building in its own right. In a sense it is one of the first centrally planned buildings of the Renaissance, but this is only true in a very general way. It is square in plan, but what is more important is the fact that the walls are equal in height to the sides of the square plan so that the building as a whole forms a perfect cube. On one side, the wall is divided into three, the central third being opened up to provide the entrance to a small altar-room which is itself square in plan and, like the main sacristy, has a hemispherical dome over it. In this way, the Old Sacristy really consists of two related cubical blocks, although the smaller space is not a true cube, its height being conditioned by that of the main sacristy. This feeling for geometry is carried a good deal further, since the section shows that the wall is divided into three equal horizontal zones, the two lower ones being the top and bottom halves of the square wall divided by the entablature. Because the dome which covers the sacristy is internally a hemisphere, its radius is necessarily one-half the width of the wall, so that the three equal zones are quite clearly visible. Like the arrangement of the chapels on plan this very simple arithmetical proportion is the essence of the whole design, but superimposed on to it are some complicated perspective effects which are partly Brunelleschi's and partly, in all probability, Donatello's. This is because the dome is carried on pendentives – spherical triangles which project forwards from the corners of the walls so that the square plan is transformed into a circle at the springing of the dome. The use of pendentives was first fully exploited in Byzantine architecture, one of the greatest examples being the church of Hagia Sophia in Constantinople; but Brunelleschi could hardly have seen any of

40

these and must have worked out the constructional system from a study of Roman remains.[6] The forward-curving surfaces of the pendentives are exploited by Donatello in his decorative system since the roundels with which Brunelleschi decorated the surfaces are treated as though they were portholes, and the spectator's eye looks through them on to a scene which is in sharp perspective. The rest of Brunelleschi's decoration consists of pilasters carrying a rather decorated entablature, similar in style to the modified Roman forms used by him in the loggia of the Foundling Hospital. The circles and half-circles are proportioned to the basic elements of the design.

The difficulty Brunelleschi encountered in fitting these classical [17] forms into his mathematically determined spaces can be seen in the corners, where the two pilasters of an outward angle have to be condensed into a fragmentary strip in the opposite, re-entrant, angles, because there is no space for a fully extended pilaster. Similar difficulties can also be seen where a pilaster is bent round an angle, or where a corbel has to appear to support a long entablature where it is not possible to place a pilaster. The same rather experimental approach is visible in the dome which is externally in section rather like the [18] lantern of the Baptistry, since it consists of a high drum with a conical tiled roof above it. Internally, however, it is a true classical hemisphere, although it is supported on ribs like those used in the Cathedral. This type, known for obvious reasons as an umbrella dome, was always used by Brunelleschi and by most of his followers until the sixteenth century. The dome is lighted by windows which appear from outside to be in the drum and from the inside to be at the base of the gores between the ribs.

Although the design for the rest of the church seems to have been established as early as about 1419, work was not resumed until about 1442, and it was not completed until long after Brunelleschi's death in 1446. One major change was made in the revision of the early 1440s, rendered necessary by the need for still more chapels. These were obtained by knocking out the wall on the outsides of the aisles and extending the aisles to north and south by spaces which are rectangular, and exactly half the area of the square bays of the aisles, which in their turn are exactly one-quarter the area of the crossing square unit. Cutting through the wall leads also to some further perspective effects since anyone in the centre of the nave finds himself looking through the main arcade and then through the round-headed

41

archway of the chapel entrance to the rear wall of the chapel, so that a succession of diminishing openings can be apprehended as a sequence of related shapes. The basic type of the church is similar to that of Sta Croce in section, as well as in plan, since the nave has a flat roof rising above the aisles, and the aisles in S. Lorenzo have simple domes. This is the type of Early Christian basilicas, and the similarities between the capitals used by Brunelleschi and those of a Romanesque church such as SS. Apostoli in Florence can hardly be coincidental. Again, Brunelleschi experienced difficulties with the proportions in S. Lorenzo which he did not experience in the later church of Sto [25] Spirito, where the same type of plan is worked out in a more coherent manner. One such difficulty may be seen in the use of dosserets above the capitals of the nave arcade. This arose because the domical vaults of the aisles are supported on pilasters on the one side and the columns of the nave on the other. The pilasters and columns must necessarily

42

FLORENCE, S. LORENZO
by Brunelleschi,
begun 1419

17, 18 Interior and section
of the Old Sacristy

19 Nave

20 Plan

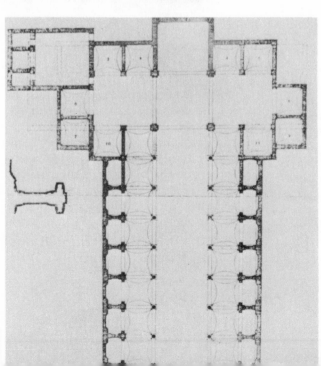

be the same height, but, because there is a raised floor at the entrance to the chapels, the pilasters stand higher than the columns and a space was therefore left between the top of the column and the bottom of the arch. A sixteenth-century architect would simply have raised the column on a base, but Brunelleschi, perhaps following a Roman or Byzantine prototype, used a dosseret to fill this space, just as he had done in the loggia of the Foundling Hospital.

Sto Spirito not only provides new and more satisfactory solutions to some of the problems encountered in S. Lorenzo, but also shows purely stylistic differences from the earlier church. These differences seem to go back to a change in Brunelleschi's style which can be dated with fair certainty to the mid 1430s, and was very probably due to a fresh visit to Rome. One of his most famous works is the Chapter House of the convent attached to Sta Croce, a small building in the [21–23] cloister known generally as the Pazzi Chapel. It was for long considered to be Brunelleschi's first work, but this was due to a mistaken interpretation of Vasari; the building is in fact a half-way house on the verge of the stylistic changes of the 1430s. The first documents which mention the chapel are of 1429, and a contract was drawn up in 1429/30 which led to a plan of 1430 or possibly of 1433. The building was not finished for forty years and the exterior is not as Brunelleschi wished it to be. The plan is a more complicated version of the Old Sacristy; that is, a central square with a dome over it, one side of which is opened to form a smaller, square, choir. The Pazzi Chapel is more sophisticated in its planning, since the square of the choir is balanced by a square vestibule which is extended on either side to match the lateral extensions or 'transepts' attached to the central space. In this way, each of the four sides of the main square is modified, and each part retains a mathematical relationship to the original unit. The spatial feeling is far more complicated than in the Old Sacristy, because the entrance vestibule has a heavy barrel-vault with a central saucer-domed space. This forms the entrance to the chapel, which has a large ribbed dome over it. The main chapel also has an extension at either side, barrel-vaulted and parallel to the corresponding portions of the entrance vestibule. Finally, the choir space repeats the smaller entrance dome beyond the main one. The treatment of the decoration, which includes some sculpture attributed to Brunelleschi himself, again shows his experimental approach to Roman architecture as well as his desire to use colouristic effects of the type traditional in Florence.

44

FLORENCE, STA CROCE, THE PAZZI CHAPEL
by Brunelleschi, 1430 or later

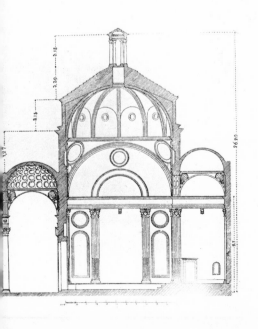

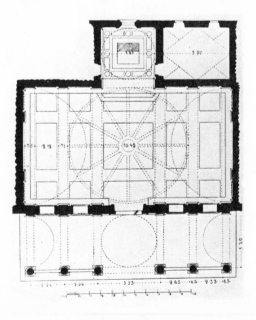

The angles are still a cause of great difficulty, with fragmentary pilasters on the one hand and bent pilasters on the other. The style of this building is very close to that of the Old Sacristy, though obviously more sophisticated. A problem arises in connection with the façade, much of which is small and ineffective, both in detail and in the feeling for proportion, though the lower part of it consists of splendidly heavy columns supporting the barrel-vault of the inside of the vestibule. This is very heavy and classical in feeling – far more so than the open, airy, quality of the loggia of the Foundling Hospital. The main dome and the dome of the portico are now known to be dated 1459 and 1461 – after Brunelleschi's death. The lower part may represent the style of his last years: this Roman quality is typical of his late work and may well be due to a renewed contact with classical antiquity.

There are no payments known to have been made to Brunelleschi in Florence between December 1432 and July 1434. It is known that Donatello was in Rome in 1432/3 and Vasari implies that Donatello and Brunelleschi visited Rome together, spending some time there in search of Roman antiquities. This assumption can be confirmed by the [24] style of works like the church of Sta Maria degli Angeli in Florence,

24 Florence, Sta Maria degli Angeli. Plan of c. 1434. Drawing by G. da Sangallo after Brunelleschi

begun in 1434 and abandoned, unfinished, in 1437. The plan is the first true central plan of the fifteenth century and derives directly from the Temple of 'Minerva Medica' in Rome. It consists of a central domed octagon – the shape of Brunelleschi's Cathedral dome – surrounded by a ring of chapels opening off the sides. It is conceived on an entirely different principle from Brunelleschi's earlier work, such as the Old Sacristy or the Pazzi Chapel, since the forms are now thought of as solid sculptural masses with the air flowing round them, whereas in the earlier work they are thought of as flat planes having geometrical relationships one to another but lacking in any plastic quality. In the same way, so far as we can reconstruct it, the dome seems to have been massively classical and based on the type represented by the Pantheon, quite different from his earlier ribbed forms. Since this building was begun immediately after the putative journey to Rome, it seems to provide very strong stylistic confirmation for a renewed classical influence; and this late style can be found in all the works datable after 1434, such as the lantern of the Cathedral, the exedrae of the Cathedral and, above all, the church of Sto Spirito.

The Basilica of Sto Spirito is basically very similar to S. Lorenzo,　　[25, 26] and the two churches between them became exemplars of the Brunelleschian style. Sto Spirito, however, shows certain points of difference from S. Lorenzo and is an example of Brunelleschi's latest and most maturely classical style. It lies in the poorer quarter beyond the Arno where a church is known to have existed on this spot since about 1250. Brunelleschi's design for rebuilding it was approved by a commission in 1434, and, after some money had been collected, the foundation-stone was laid in 1436. Very little, however, was done; and when Brunelleschi died ten years later the first column was on the site, but the church was not finished until 1482, after a long controversy which resulted in some alterations to the original design. These alterations are known to us largely through the anonymous Life of Brunelleschi which is our principal source of information about his career. So far as we can make out, there should have been four main doors at the west end where there are now three; the system of domical aisle bays which runs right round the eastern end of the church should have been continued behind the west wall so that each door opened into one of the small square bays; and, finally, the outside line of the church ought to have been a rather curious shape with the semicircular walls of the side chapels expressed as convex curves

[25] on the outside, instead of being filled in to form a straight wall, as they now are. It is highly likely that these alterations were made by the later architects contrary to Brunelleschi's desires, since it would seem that this rather curious curved wall-system was probably inspired by part of the Lateran Basilica in Rome, which once had such a feature, and which Brunelleschi probably thought was Early Christian. In the same way, the idea of a continuous ring of small domed spaces forming an internal prelude to the larger spaces of the nave, choir, and transepts, fits in very well with the spatial feeling of Brunelleschi's later works and it seems to be confirmed by the fact that the space left blank on the present plan is exactly large enough for the two extra bays. We know that a model was made by Brunelleschi and was approved in 1434, but the plans were modified some ten years later so that in their final form they truly represent the style of Brunelleschi's last years.

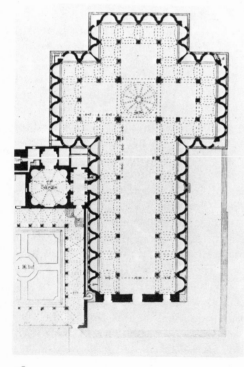

FLORENCE, STO SPIRITO
by Brunelleschi,
1434 or later

25 Plan   26 Nave

Although the plan of Sto Spirito differs from that of S. Lorenzo, the real contrast between the two churches is best experienced in three dimensions when standing inside them. Even on plan it can be seen that the rectangular forms of S. Lorenzo are modified in Sto Spirito, as in all Brunelleschi's later works, into something far more sculptural in feeling. Where in S. Lorenzo the small chapels are rectangles with flat pilasters set at the openings as responds to the columns, in Sto Spirito the semicircular niches of the chapel forms are repeated as counter curves in the half-columns at the entrances to the chapels, which serve as responds to the columns in the nave. Again, the proportions inside the church are more fully worked out, and the slightly awkward proportion in S. Lorenzo formed by the height of the arcade in relation to the height of the clerestory above it (roughly 3:2) is much more satisfactorily treated in Sto Spirito, where the arcade height is the same as the clerestory height. The bays of the aisles have domical vaults, the roof of the nave is flat and painted to represent coffering; but the aisle bays are now half the height of the nave bays as well as half their width, and this, once again, can be traced back to the tenth-century church of SS. Apostoli which has the same 1:2 proportion. The splendid spatial effect created by the great ring of columns running round the whole church is perhaps hardly to be appreciated except by actually walking through it, but it is certainly the case that it has a richness and truly Roman grandeur, not to be found in Brunelleschi's earlier works, which makes the church of Sto Spirito a fitting conclusion to his career. The imitators who succeeded him were not capable of grasping the mathematical severity combined with sculptural richness of the late buildings and they tended to choose works of his earlier period, such as the Foundling Hospital, as examples for imitation. A case in point is the Badia at Fiesole, just outside Florence, which was not begun until after Brunelleschi's death, but which is closer to the work of the 1420s than to any of the buildings of his later style.

[19]

[26]

50

CHAPTER THREE

Alberti

The other major architect of the earlier part of the fifteenth century was Leon Battista Alberti who was, however, as different as possible from Brunelleschi; he was a man to whom architecture represented only one activity among many. Alberti was one of the greatest scholars of his age, whereas we know that Brunelleschi was unable to read Latin and was obviously a man who liked to work out things for himself. Alberti was born in Genoa, very probably in 1404, an illegitimate member of an important Florentine merchant family which was temporarily in exile. The young Alberti was given an excellent education, first at the University of Padua, where at a very early age he acquired a mastery of Greek and Latin, and later at the University of Bologna, where he studied law. When his father died he was supported by two uncles, both of whom were priests, since it was quite evident that the young man was developing into a prodigy, and indeed at the age of twenty he wrote a Latin comedy which for a short time passed as genuinely antique. This was perhaps less difficult in the fifteenth century than it would be now, since these were the very years when a small number of humanist scholars were rediscovering a vast number of classical manuscripts and there was nothing very strange in the discovery of a comedy which purported to be antique. Alberti soon met most of the greater humanists of the next generation including, in all probability, the future Nicholas V, the first·humanist Pope and later Alberti's employer. About 1428, or perhaps a little earlier, the banishment of his family was revoked and he went to Florence where he met Brunelleschi and probably also Donatello and Ghiberti. In his book on painting he mentions Masaccio as well, so it is quite evident that he moved in the same kind of advanced artistic circles in Florence as the humanist circles he was accustomed to in Padua and Bologna. The dedication of his book is one of the few pieces of evidence for a connection between humanist ideas and the arts. Soon after this he took minor orders and entered the Papal Civil Service, as did many humanists of that period. He travelled widely, and, in the early 1430s, while living in Rome, he began to make an intensive study of the ruins of classical antiquity. This, however, was approached in an entirely different way from Brunelleschi's study of the same ruins. Brunelleschi was primarily concerned with discovering how the Romans had been able to build on an enormous scale and to roof vast spaces; in other words, he was interested in classical architecture from a purely structural point of view. Alberti, who almost always employed an assistant to do the actual building for him, was probably incapable of understanding the structural system of Roman architecture and certainly was not very interested in it. He was, however, the first theorist of the new humanist art, and his study of classical ruins was for the purpose of deducing what he imagined to be the immutable rules governing the arts. He wrote three treatises – on painting, sculpture, and architecture – and in each case we see that not only is his prose modelled on Ciceronian Latin, but the whole cast of his mind is to seek for antique exemplars which can be modified to suit contemporary circumstances. In 1434 he returned to Florence and there began work on the first of his treatises on the arts, the short *Della Pittura*, dealing with the theoretical basis of painting and dedicated to Brunelleschi, Donatello, Ghiberti, Luca della Robbia, and Masaccio, the most formidable combination of artists then to be found. (Masaccio, of course, was dead before 1434, but all the others were at the height of their careers.) *Della Pittura* was finished in 1435 and shows Alberti's scientific interest in problems of proportion and perspective. Much space is devoted to the problem of the representation on a plane surface of objects assumed to be at varying distances, and to the problem of maintaining an equal scale of diminution between them. This is fundamentally a rational and naturalistic approach to the arts, and the same preconceptions can be found in his book on the theory of architecture and his pamphlet on sculpture.

Alberti's architectural interests began in the 1440s – that is, in the last years of Brunelleschi's lifetime – and it was probably then that he began to compose his greatest theoretical work, the ten books on architecture, *De re aedificatoria*, of which a version was presented to Pope Nicholas V in 1452, but which Alberti probably continued to modify until his death in 1472. We know from an anonymous Life (which may be an autobiography) that Alberti practised all three arts, but we have no certain paintings or sculpture by him, and his reputation as an artist rests equally on his writings and on his buildings.

The obvious classical model for Alberti's book on architecture was the work of Vitruvius, the only technical treatise on the arts to have come down to us from classical antiquity. In fact, a manuscript of Vitruvius was rediscovered rather dramatically by the humanist Poggio about 1415, although knowledge of the treatise had never been entirely lost. It is, however, certain that Alberti was the first man to make real use of the text of Vitruvius since it was, and is, extremely corrupt and in parts entirely unintelligible. Alberti's purpose, therefore, was to write on the basic principles of architecture as Vitruvius had done before him, and to use Vitruvius as a guide without in any way copying him. Much of Alberti's treatise is clearly recognizable as a product of the early Humanist Age, with its emphasis on the development of the individual through the cultivation of the will, the restraint of feeling, and the development of one's own capacity in order to secure the public good. This very Roman conception of the individual is characteristic of the early fifteenth century, but it is slightly surprising to find Alberti referring to 'the temples' and 'the gods' when he means churches, God, and the Saints. This rather self-conscious Latin usage has led to a fundamental misconception of Alberti's ideas, since it is quite clear that in spite of his insistence on the glories of antiquity and the supremacy of antique art, he is nevertheless thinking entirely within a Christian framework.

Alberti gives the first consistent theory of the use of the five orders since classical times. He has a design for a town plan and for a series of houses suited to the different classes. He also has a coherent theory of beauty and ornament in architecture which depends basically on a mathematical system of harmonic proportions, since he defines beauty as 'a harmony and concord of all the parts, so that nothing could be added or subtracted except for the worse'. This beauty can, rather illogically, be improved by ornament which is superimposed on harmonic proportion, and the principal ornament of architecture is the column. It is evident, therefore, that Alberti was ignorant of the essentially functional nature of the column in Greek architecture, and, like some of the Roman architects, he regarded it as a mere ornament on the load-bearing wall.

His first works were a palace in Florence for the Rucellai family, and a church which he rebuilt for Sigismondo Malatesta, the tyrant of Rimini. It is likely that the Palazzo Rucellai was the first to be erected, but it will be more convenient to consider it in the next chapter along with other Florentine palaces of the fifteenth century. The church in Rimini was an old one dedicated to St Francis, but it is now more usually known as the Tempio Malatestiano since it was rebuilt from about 1446 onwards by Sigismondo with the intention of making it a memorial to himself, to his wife Isotta, and to the members of his court. The idea of rebuilding the church to the glory of God was clearly a very secondary consideration in Sigismondo's [27] mind. The importance of the Tempio Malatestiano at Rimini in the history of architecture lies in the fact that it is the first modern example of a classical solution to the problem presented by the western façade of a normal Christian church; that is, a high central nave with a lower aisle on either side, each covered by a lean-to roof. The rather awkward shape thus produced was not a common classical form, since the traditional classical temple consisted of a portico standing in front of a single cella. The Gothic solution of western towers, common in France and England, was hardly ever used in Italy and Alberti had therefore no immediate prototype to draw on. The fact that the Tempio Malatestiano was so patently dedicated to the glory of an earthly prince may well have suggested the solution adopted, which was to recast the old west end of the church into a form based upon the classical triumphal arch, so that the idea of victory over death is implied in the choice of a triumphal arch at the entrance to the church. Most classical examples consist either of a single arch flanked by columns – there is such an Arch of Augustus in Rimini itself – or are of a tripartite form with a large central arch and small ones on either side separated by columns. The most famous example of this, and one which was certainly very well known to Alberti, is the Arch of Constantine in Rome. This was undoubtedly the original model for the church at Rimini although many of the details are taken directly from the Arch of Augustus. The Arch of Constantine, however, only provided a solution to the problem presented by the different sizes of nave and aisles. Alberti was still faced with the problem of the greater height of the nave, and, since triumphal arches are invariably of a single storey with perhaps an attic, some other form had to be found and adapted for the upper part of the building. In fact the building was never completed and the interior is still largely Gothic, but it is possible to deduce Alberti's intentions from the fragment which exists, and from a medal cast

54

27 Rimini, the Tempio Malatestiano. Façade by Alberti, 1446 and later

by Matteo de' Pasti about 1450. Matteo was Alberti's assistant at Rimini and was responsible for most of the actual building. A letter, recently rediscovered, from Alberti to Matteo de' Pasti of 18 November 1454 explains clearly some of Alberti's ideas, and the medal shows his proposed solution for the upper storey. It also proves that he intended to build a very large dome, hemispherical in shape, like the Pantheon, but carried on ribs, like Brunelleschi's Cathedral. The solution for the upper part of the façade was to repeat the large arched opening above the doorway, using it as a window and flanking it with columns (or rather pilasters), the bases of which can be seen on the building as it exists. The roofs of the aisles were to be masked by low segmental screening walls with decorative motifs on them. This general system, with the use of two orders one above the other in the centre, became one of the commonest forms in Western church architecture. In the letter written to Matteo de' Pasti, he explains this, saying:

> Remember and bear well in mind that in the model, on the right and left sides along the edge of the roof, there is a thing like this (*here is a little drawing of the decorative detail*) and I told you I am putting it there to conceal that part of the roof that will be put on inside the church, since one cannot reduce the internal width with my façade, and the object must be to improve what is already built and not to spoil what is yet to be done. You can see where the sizes and proportions of the pilasters come from: if you alter anything you will spoil all that harmony. . . .

Elsewhere in the same letter he also states his faith in a rationalistic architecture, as well as in the precedents provided by antiquity, when he says: 'but as for what you tell me Manetto says about cupolas having to be twice as high as they are wide, I for my part have more faith in the men who built the Baths and the Pantheon and all those noble edifices than I have in him, and a great deal more in reason than in any man'.

Classical as his intentions were, the detail in the Tempio Malatestiano is quite often much closer to Venetian Gothic forms than to Roman antiquity. This was probably due to the fact that Alberti was designing the building by correspondence, and Matteo and the masons on the spot were using the northern decorative forms most familiar to them.

The small Rucellai Chapel in Florence, finished in 1467, is very much more classical in its detail than the Tempio Malatestiano, perhaps owing to the classical forms used by Brunelleschi and already more familiar to Florentine masons than to those in the rest of Italy. It is therefore with some surprise that the façade of the great [28] Florentine church of Sta Maria Novella is seen to be dated 1470. This was also commissioned by the Rucellai family, but it is now known that the façade was begun in 1458. Like the Tempio Malatestiano, the design was conditioned by the existing building, and in this case it has been suggested that Alberti was deliberately using some of the Gothic forms of the older parts of the building and

28 Florence, Sta Maria Novella. Façade by Alberti, begun 1458

that he intended to compromise with, or even to reconstruct, the older style. Because of its less novel (and therefore more acceptable) character the façade of Sta Maria Novella was widely copied by later architects, the more so since it provided a model 'antique' façade for a Gothic type of church. What Alberti does is to divide the whole space in such a way that the height of the building is equal to its width, thereby forming a single large square. This is then further subdivided half-way up its height by the base of the scroll forms which he used to mask the aisles. The lower part of the façade, divided by the main door, thus forms two squares, each of which is one quarter of the area of the large square. The upper storey screening the end of the nave and crowned by a classical triangular pediment is of exactly the same size as the two lower squares below it. This mathematical division into proportions as simple as 1:1, 1:2, 1:4, is characteristic of all Alberti's work, and it is really this dependence on mathematics in both Brunelleschi and Alberti which marks the decisive distinction between them and their predecessors. In his treatise Alberti frequently adverts to the necessity for such simple harmonic proportions and this is obviously what he meant in the letter to Matteo de' Pasti when he said 'if you alter anything you will spoil all that harmony'.

Towards the end of his life Alberti designed two more churches, both in Mantua and both begun by him without any existing building to modify his designs. They are of great importance for future church building because each represents one of the two main types, [30, 32] S. Sebastiano being a Greek cross in plan and S. Andrea a Latin cross. S. Sebastiano was begun in 1460 but was still unfinished when Alberti died in 1472. The present building is an incorrect restoration and the diagram shown in plate 29 is a reconstruction proposed by Professor Wittkower.[7] This clearly shows almost all of the theoretical requirements laid down by Alberti in his treatise. It has a high flight of steps because Alberti thought that churches ought to stand on a high base isolated from the world around them. It has six pilasters supporting an entablature – the existing building has the entablature but only four pilasters – because in this instance Alberti was deliberately using the classical temple-front type, since the plan eliminated aisles.

58

The plan itself is perhaps more important even than the façade, for it is the first of a long series of Greek cross structures many of which date from the sixteenth century. In theory Alberti regarded the centrally planned church, of which the Greek cross is a good example, as being a perfect form in itself and symbolizing therefore the perfection of God. On the other hand, it is likely that he was also influenced by Early Christian churches, and the near-by city of Ravenna provides at least two possible prototypes – the Mausoleum of Galla Placidia of about 450 and the church of Sta Croce of about the same date.[8] Nevertheless, the Greek cross plan was never very popular, partly because of the difficulty of housing a congregation, and Alberti's other church in Mantua provided a more acceptable model for later architects.

S. Andrea was designed only two years before Alberti died: the [31–33] building was not even begun until 1472, and Alberti's ideas were carried out by an assistant, but much of the church was not completed until the eighteenth century and the present aspect of the façade is as Alberti intended it only as far as the pediment. The plan is of the more traditional Latin cross type which had already been used by Brunelleschi in his two Florentine churches, but with one essential difference. In Brunelleschi's churches the aisles are separated from the naves only by slender columns, and when one stands in the nave or the aisles the main axial direction is towards the altar at the east end. In S. Andrea there are no aisles but a series of alternating large and

MANTUA,
S. SEBASTIANO
by Alberti,
begun 1460

29 Reconstruction of
façade by R. Wittkower

30 Plan

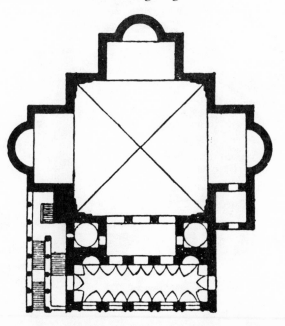

small spaces opening off the nave at right angles to it. The larger spaces are used as chapels, and, standing in the nave, the spectator therefore has two axial directions, one of which consists of a small-large-small rhythm running laterally down the nave walls and the other longitudinal, which is concentrated towards the east end, is provided by the tunnel-like character of the nave itself.

The principal reason for this great spatial difference between the Brunelleschian and Albertian types lies in the fact that Alberti was consciously modelling his interior on Roman prototypes. The nave of S. Andrea, which is very dark, has a barrel-vault with painted coffers, some 56 feet wide, by far the largest and heaviest erected since classical times. The immense weight of this vault must of necessity be carried on very large supports, stronger than the columns used in Brunelleschi's type of church. Alberti therefore used the prototype provided by such Roman buildings as the Baths of Diocletian or the Basilica of Constantine, in which enormous abutments carried the

MANTUA, S. ANDREA   by Alberti, designed 1470

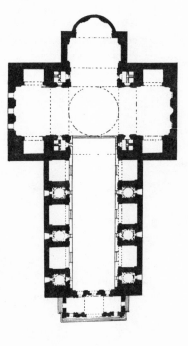

31 Façade   32 Plan

33 Nave

weight of the vaulting, but at the same time could be hollowed out to form openings at right angles to the main axes. Thus the vast piers of S. Andrea can be hollowed out into small and large chapel spaces without impairing their resistance to the thrust of the vault. This type of Latin cross plan, with its rhythmic alternation and the possibility of using a stone-vaulted roof, was very widely copied in the later sixteenth century, particularly under the influence of Vignola and of the Jesuits, who adapted the form for the very numerous churches they built in the seventeenth century.

[148]

A glance at the façade shows that Alberti was able to modify his internal system and to repeat it on the exterior, combining it with the type of classical temple front that he had already used for S. Sebastiano. The façade of S. Andrea consists of an interlocking of a classical triumphal arch (this time of the single arch type) with a classical temple front. The temple front is formed by the four large pilasters on high bases, carrying a shallow triangular pediment above them; the triumphal arch consists of the large round-headed opening immediately below the pediment, flanked by pilasters and with its own entablature running behind the pilasters of the temple front. This results in a small opening at ground level between two pilasters, followed by a large round-headed opening, and then a repetition of the smaller doorway. This is the same as the rhythmic alternation of the large and small chapels, the basic feature of the interior, and derives from the Arch of Septimius Severus in Rome.

In these later buildings Alberti is clearly dependent on Roman prototypes, but he does not allow himself to be bound by them, and this same detached attitude to the buildings of antiquity can be found in many of the passages of his treatise. Obviously he regards the architecture of the Romans as being in every way superior to the efforts of the architects in the generations immediately preceding his own, but it is clear that he also feels that men like Brunelleschi (or himself) were capable of using the rules which they could deduce from classical architecture for different purposes without slavish imitation. It should be remembered that Alberti was not the only major archaeologically minded artist in Mantua at this moment, since his patron Ludovico Gonzaga employed as his Court Painter Andrea Mantegna. The *Adoration* (now in the Uffizi) or the decorations in the Camera degli Sposi in the Palazzo Gonzaga at Mantua are contemporary with Alberti's churches.

CHAPTER FOUR

Palace design in Florence, Venice and elsewhere

The development of society in Italy was very different from the rest of Europe. Almost the whole of the civilized world in the thirteenth and fourteenth centuries was governed by a conception of society which was more or less feudalistic, and which therefore tended to concentrate power in the hands of individual lords in the country-side, each based on his own castle and ruling in virtue of the small private army that he maintained, whereas in Italy the basis of society depended partly on the Church and partly on the very early develop-ment of towns. The towns established by the Romans continued to be the most important centres in the country and, indeed, there are many small towns in Italy which have a continuous record of over two thousand years of independent existence. The rise of the merchant classes was particularly noticeable in some of the larger towns such as Florence, and it was to Florence that, during the fifteenth century, the economic leadership of the country was to pass. The actual structure of Italian politics was inordinately complicated since there were two major political parties, the Guelfs and the Ghibellines; and in theory the Guelf party (which was further subdivided into Black and White Guelfs) supported the idea of the temporal dominion of the Papacy as against the claims put forward in the name of what still called itself the Holy Roman Empire. The Ghibellines held to the principle of the supremacy of the Emperor in all temporal affairs, but these theoretical positions were modified in an almost infinite number of ways. For example, the city of Florence, though techni-cally Guelf, was far from subservient to the Papacy, whereas the city of Siena, the traditional enemy of Florence, was technically Ghibelline though very much more clerical in its politics. As a very rough generalization it may also be said that the Ghibelline Sienese tended to encourage an aristocratic semi-feudal form of society where the Guelf Florentines based their conception of society on a merchant oligarchy. A new Florentine Republic was established in the year 1250, and in 1293 the Ordinances of Justice were drawn up as a sort of Republican Constitution. Political power was specifically

63

conferred on the great corporations or guilds, of which there were twenty-one in all. Seven of these, known as the Arti Maggiori, were the leaders both politically and economically while the other fourteen, the Arti Minori, were used to offset the balance of power among the seven greater guilds. These seven were the Lawyers (Giudici e Notai), the Cloth Manufacturers (the Arte della Lana), the Cloth Finishers (Calimala), the Silk Workers (Seta), the Bankers and Moneychangers (Cambio), the Furriers (Pellicciai), and the Doctors and Apothecaries. This last – the Medici e Speziali – was the guild to which the painters belonged, since in theory colours were imported drugs, and drugs were the affair of apothecaries. All these greater guilds contained a number of craftsmen from related crafts – for example, the Goldsmiths were included in the Guild of Silk – so that in fact membership of the greater guilds was more widely spread than might seem to be the case.[9] On the other hand, the first four of the greater guilds, Giudici e Notai, Lana, Calimala and Cambio, had the effective power since the economic life of the city depended very largely on the cloth trade and on the international finance of which the Florentines, who invented double entry book-keeping, were the first exponents in Europe. The concentration of power was carried still further, since the greater guilds tended to be dominated by individual families, many of whom were both extremely rich and extremely ramified. In the fifteenth century every great Florentine family business had agents not only elsewhere in Italy but commonly in Bruges and London as well. This small number of very powerful families was opposed by a very large proportion of the population of Florence, the so-called *Popolo Minuto*, the 'little people' who had no political power at all. There can be no greater error than to imagine that Florence, because it had no king and no aristocracy, resembled a modern democracy in any way whatever. In fact, the political discontents of the majority of the population tended to express themselves in outbursts of rioting of which the most famous was the Ciompi Revolt of 1378, when the unskilled wool-workers struck for better working conditions. As a result of these periodic outbursts of violence most of the houses of the wealthier families tended to become semi-fortified, and this trend was much increased by the fact that virtually every family lived over its business premises. Unlike the feudal nobility living in castles in the remote countryside, the Florentine merchant had to live on top of his work and he therefore preferred to build a palace which could simultaneously be an office and a warehouse. Once more this was nothing new, for the combination of shops and warehouses with flats above them was derived directly from ancient Rome. What makes the Florentine palace architecturally important is the fact that at the end of the fourteenth and beginning of the fifteenth centuries a special architectural type was established which was followed, and modified where necessary, in the rest of Italy. There are some good examples of public buildings of this type dating from the late thirteenth century, the most famous being the Palazzo Vecchio (or Palazzo della Signoria) and the Bargello, both in Florence. The Palazzo della Signoria, as its name implies, was the Town Hall and dates from 1298 to 1340, with later alterations and additions. The design is attributed to Arnolfo di Cambio. The Bargello, begun in 1255, was the official residence of the Podestà or Chief Magistrate. By a sensible convention, the Podestà was always someone who was not a member of one of the leading Florentine families. As he was usually a foreigner it was necessary to provide him with an official residence and this also served as a court of justice and a prison. Both the Bargello and the Palazzo Vecchio, for obvious reasons, present a strongly fortified appearance from the street and both have bell-towers, for the ringing of the tocsin was an official means of giving warning or causing the citizens to gather. For the rest, the design is kept quite simple; a certain amount of rustication, with windows made up of two lights set in a pointed arch and separated by a colonette, and with a plain string-course marking the storeys. In both cases the ground-floor windows are small and high up, and in both cases also the design of the building is that of a rectangle enclosing a central court, roughly square in plan, which serves as a means of obtaining light and air, and which also usually has a well, so that in the event of a day or two of rioting the building had its own water supply and the outside windows could be closed and barred.

This general type underlies the design of most of the major palaces, a very good example of which is the Palazzo Davanzati, [34] now a Museum of Furniture and Decoration. This palace dates from the late fourteenth century, and its derivation from the classical type is at once apparent since it consists of a large ground floor taken up by the shop and warehouse quarters with the living quarters set above them. It is slightly different from the majority of palaces of this type in that it has only a staircase court, because it is on a restricted site, and the very large loggia on the top floor provides somewhere for the family to sit on summer evenings. The building consists of five storeys, including the loggia, of which the first four diminish in size upwards, so that there is a graded proportion between each of the storeys, the ground floor being not only the largest but also marked by rusticated stonework giving it an air of greater solidity. The three great warehouse openings set in slightly pointed arches are arranged symmetrically with small mezzanine windows above them. The remaining three storeys have five windows arranged symmetrically above the three great openings on the ground floor, and it is in these rooms that the family lived. The first floor, or *piano nobile*, is obviously the best, because it is above the noise and dust of the street, but not as hot as the rooms under the roof, and it was for this reason that it was called *piano nobile*, since the main public rooms and the apartments of the head of the family were always put there. The next floor upwards was usually occupied by children and various less-important members of the family, while the top floor, hot in summer and cold in winter, was given to the servants. This general arrangement, which can be seen in almost exactly the same form in Roman towns such as Ostia, had been worked out at least fourteen hundred years earlier and is a form which can still be seen in modern Italian buildings. From the point of view of the architect, therefore, the problem was not a functional one but a matter of design, and it was here that the greatest advances were made in the fifteenth century. Brunelleschi is not known to have designed a single surviving palace for a private family and Alberti designed only one, but their influence determined the type which was established in Florence and spread outwards from there.

In 1433 a great political crisis culminated in the expulsion from Florence of Cosimo de' Medici and his family. He went to Venice taking with him his family bank. Within a year, the flight of capital from Florence was such that the ban of exile was lifted and in 1434 Cosimo returned to Florence to become its virtual ruler for the next thirty years. Cosimo himself was extremely careful to retain the reality of power without ever appearing to do so. He was never more, in theory, than a private citizen, but in fact he manipulated the politics of Florence in two simple but subtle ways. The first was by means of the smaller guilds. Cosimo realized that the greater

34 Florence,
Palazzo Davanzati.
Late 14th century

guilds contained many men, like the Albizzi family, who were
intensely jealous of him; and he therefore did not seek to dominate
the greater guilds directly. What he did was to place members of his
family, sons-in-law and others, into positions of authority in the
smaller guilds. This meant that, for example, the Innkeepers' Guild
felt that they had a powerful ally against the oppression of the greater
guilds, and at the same time they were bound to the fortunes of the
Medici family. Cosimo was thus able to rely on the cumulative
political pressure which could be brought by a federation of the
smaller guilds, coupled with the fact that many members of the
greater guilds, though hating him personally, realized that a period

of stable government was essential for the economic progress of the city. Cosimo's other main weapon was equally subtle, but perhaps less morally defensible. This was the manipulation of a kind of income tax, and it soon became noted that the assessments made varied greatly, according to whether the person in question supported or opposed Cosimo's policies. Unlike so many other fifteenth-century politicians Cosimo de' Medici probably never murdered anybody: he found it just as effective to render enemies bankrupt.

One result of Cosimo's long domination, which was continued by his son and grandson almost to the end of the century, was that from about 1434 onwards many families were able to spend in building elaborate palaces money and energy which would otherwise have been wasted in political feuding. As one might expect, the Palazzo Medici is itself the leading example of this new type of domestic architecture. There is a story, which may well be true, that Cosimo de' Medici, who was a personal friend of Brunelleschi, asked him to design a new palace for the family. Brunelleschi, who had almost no opportunity for such domestic work, was delighted and made a very elaborate model of a superb palace. Cosimo, however, looked at it and remarked that it was too elaborate and that 'envy is a plant one should never water'. According to the story, Brunelleschi was so incensed that he smashed the model. It is certainly true that the architect of the Medici family was not Brunelleschi but Michelozzo Michelozzi (1396–1472). Michelozzo had been in partnership with Donatello and was profoundly influenced by Brunelleschi, so that when he devoted himself to architecture, from about 1434, his style [35-37] was very largely formed on Brunelleschian principles. To this extent, therefore, it is possible to say that the Palazzo Medici shows the influence of Brunelleschi's ideas on palace design. Building began in 1444 and was completed about twenty years later, the chapel being finished about 1459. On the outside the only significant modification made later was the filling in of the open arches at the angles with [35] windows designed by Michelangelo in the early sixteenth century, and the enormous increase in size of the palace down Via Larga when it was bought by the Riccardi in the early eighteenth century. By comparison with the Palazzo Davanzati it can be seen at once that the Palazzo Medici design makes no startling innovations, yet it embodies the new principles of symmetry and mathematical arrangement. There are now only three storeys topped by an enormous

68

classical cornice, the purpose of which is to cast a shadow down the walls when the sun is at its highest. The same purpose was served by the projecting eaves roof of the Palazzo Davanzati at considerably less expense. The great stone cornice of the Palazzo Medici is classical in form, being based on a classical entablature, and related to the height of the entire palace. It is approximately 10 feet high and the palace wall is 83 feet. This means that the projection of the cornice has to be counterbalanced by keying the blocks back into the roof in the most elaborate and expensive manner; and all in order to obtain what many later architects would have regarded as an architectural solecism, since the cornice has no architrave or frieze below it and no columns to go with it. Furthermore, the height and projection of the cornice is related to the whole height of the palace and not to the individual storeys so that the top floor, looked at by itself, appears to be somewhat crushed. This is made more obvious when one considers the arrangement of the three separate storeys. The ground floor has round-headed openings with very strongly marked voussoirs, the outside and the inside of which are concentric and not, as in the Palazzo Davanzati, slightly pointed. These round openings are placed symmetrically in a very heavily rusticated wall, the irregular quality of which gives the ground floor a distinctly rugged appearance. Separating the ground floor and the *piano nobile* there is a small string-course in the form of a classical modillion cornice which serves also as sills for the windows of the *piano nobile*. These windows, like the openings on the ground floor, are arranged symmetrically, but they are not related to each other, so that the centres of the *piano nobile* windows do not correspond with the openings below them. The windows have voussoir patterns very similar to those below them, but the opening is divided into two lights by means of a single colonette with round-headed arches over it, a more classically expressed form of the type of two-light window in the Bargello or the Palazzo Vecchio. The storey as a whole is smaller than the ground floor and is sharply distinguished from it by the fact that the rusticated stonework has no rough bosses but consists solely of channels cut along the joints. The top storey is identical with the *piano nobile* except that it is now entirely smooth so that there is a marked gradation in the stonework through all three storeys and the optical effect is to make the palace seem even higher than it actually is.

69

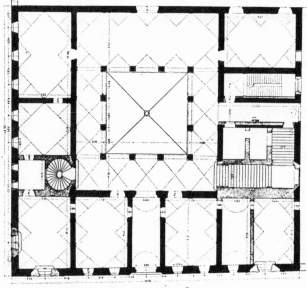

FLORENCE,
PALAZZO MEDICI
by Michelozzo, begun 1444

35 Street façade

36 Plan

37 Court

The arrangement of the inside of the palace is similar to the outside
in that it consists of a re-working of a traditional type with great
attention to proportion and symmetry. The basic shape of the building
is a hollow square with a large, open, central court which, at ground
level, forms an open arcade exactly like a monastic cloister and is of
the same type as the court in such earlier palaces as the Bargello.
The differences between the Palazzo Medici and its predecessors are [36]
all apparently small but none the less significant. For example, the
planning is now very nearly symmetrical, with the main entrance
doorway in the centre of the original front leading through a long
tunnel-like entrance into the central axis of the court. The departures
from symmetry can be seen in the plan, where it is clear that the far
end of the court is wider than the other sides and the arrangement of
the rooms is by no means strictly symmetrical on the axes. It may
be noted that the main staircases are still comparatively unimportant,
but at least they open out of the covered arcade and are not completely exposed, as was the case in many of the earlier palaces. The
idea of a grand ceremonial staircase as a principal architectural feature
was nearly another century in arriving.

It is in the disposition of the courtyard itself that Brunelleschi's influence is most clearly to be seen; at the same time it is evident that Michelozzo was far less inventive and far less sensitive an architect than Brunelleschi, since his handling of the difficulties inherent in the problem is rather unimaginative. In effect, the court of the Palazzo Medici is the façade of the Foundling Hospital bent round to form a hollow square. The sides of the square reveal at a glance their derivation from the Foundling Hospital (compare plates 16 and 37), since there is a series of round-headed arches carried on columns with a very wide frieze above them, the cornice above this frieze forming the sills of the windows of the first floor. What Michelozzo failed to realize is that by bending the straight façade of the Foundling Hospital he raised problems at the angles which he was unable to solve. In the first place, in the Foundling Hospital the ends of the façade are given apparent strength by the large pilasters supporting the entablature which runs above the round-headed openings. These pilasters are also necessary, in theory at any rate, to support the entablature. Michelozzo omits the large pilasters, since they would have coincided with the angles in his court, but by doing so he modifies the original design in three ways which between them rob his own of much of its effect. By omitting the pilasters and making the angles of the square meet on a single column, not distinguished in any way from the other columns of the arcade, he makes the angles of the court appear rather weak. The whole point of the pilaster system, apart from its apparent support of the entablature, was to provide visually strong areas to close the ends of the façade. Next, and perhaps more important, is the unfortunate effect produced by the grouping of the windows. Michelozzo used round-headed windows on the first floor similar in shape and proportion to the arches below them, and, following Brunelleschi, the centres of the windows coincide with the centres of the arches below them, so that an even and symmetrical distribution of voids is obtained. Unfortunately, by turning the arcade at right angles at each of the corners the two windows in each corner come much closer together than those in the centres of the walls, and thus the weak effect produced by the use of a single column at the angles is further accentuated by the over-close spacing of the windows. Instead of making matters better, this effect is emphasized by the entablature with its excessively high frieze which separates the tops of the arcades from the bases of

38 Florence,
Palazzo Rucellai.
After 1446 by Alberti

the windows. The very deep frieze has roundels placed below the window centres so that they also come too close together at the corners and appear too widely spaced in the centres. The problems presented by the design of such a court were comparatively slow in being solved, and in fact most of the great Florentine palaces repeat this general type for at least a century. It was outside Florence, in Rome and above all in Urbino, that these problems were first solved.

The next important palace type in Florence was provided almost immediately by Alberti's Palazzo Rucellai, begun after 1446 (?1450s). [38] It is smaller than the Palazzo Medici and was built at about the same time, so that some of the details, such as the colonettes separating the windows, resemble Michelozzo's. The Palazzo Rucellai differs essentially from the Palazzo Medici in that it is the first consistent attempt to apply the classical Orders to a palace front and, indeed, the whole building has a much more consciously antique air. It is in some ways a more sophisticated building, since it has a great variety of texture and some subtle emphases in the main bays. Unlike the Palazzo Medici, with its single entrance in the centre of the façade, the Palazzo Rucellai has two main doors so disposed that the façade is intended to be read A A B A A B A A (in fact the last 'A' bay was never built, but the beginnings are clearly visible: in fact the original façade may have been of five bays only). The bays containing the doors are very slightly wider than the other bays and are also marked by the elaborately carved coats of arms over the first-floor windows.

This alternating rhythm is itself more complex than the organization of the Palazzo Medici, but the complexity is greatly increased by the innovation of the orders, used to divide the building both horizontally and vertically. The horizontal division is accomplished by elaborately decorated entablatures carrying Rucellai badges rather than the formal decorative motifs of a correct classical order. As in the Palazzo Medici, each cornice acts as a sill for the windows. These horizontal divisions are supported by correctly proportioned pilasters, and the whole scheme is clearly derived from the Colosseum. Vitruvius mentions only four orders, since the Roman Composite seems to have been invented after his death. Alberti, however, had seen examples in Rome and, in *De re aedificatoria*, he distinguished it from the Corinthian, thus beginning the tradition of the 'five orders'. In practice he seems to have followed the precedent set by the Colosseum, where the top two storeys have Corinthian columns followed by Corinthian pilasters: in the Palazzo Rucellai the ground floor has a Tuscan-type pilaster, the *piano nobile* a rather rich form of the Corinthian (instead of Ionic), and the top floor has a simpler, more correct, type of Corinthian. He probably felt that the richer form should distinguish the *piano nobile*, but this unclassical usage is also evidence for the difficulty experienced, even by the most classical architect of the day, in distinguishing between the orders.

74

Following classical precedent, the heights of the storeys were those fixed by the heights of the pilasters, which in themselves were pre-determined by the fact that they bore a proportional relationship one to another. The ground floor is given the necessary height – since Tuscan pilasters must be shorter and heavier than the others – by the addition of a considerable base below them forming a long seat with a back to it made up of stone carved in a diamond pattern to imitate Roman *opus reticulatum*. This apparently minor detail is significant of much of Alberti's approach to classical architecture. Since he was using pilasters as the main element in the whole façade he was obviously debarred from employing graded rustication like that which Michelozzo used so effectively on the Palazzo Medici. Alberti's Palazzo has a richly textured effect owing to the contrast provided by the channelled rustication of the main wall surfaces, the emphasized channelling of the round-headed windows, and the further contrasts provided by the smooth pilasters and the *opus reticulatum* which serves as a base. It is clear, therefore, that Alberti used this diamond pattern as a means of obtaining a textural contrast at a point where he needed some form of base below the pilasters, and for this reason he adopted the diamond shapes which must have been familiar to him in ancient Roman buildings. In fact, however, *opus reticulatum* was not merely a decorative device. To the Roman architect it was the equivalent of the modern technique of reinforcing concrete. The Romans had found that large quantities of concrete can be made even stronger by the provision of some kind of rein-forcement which holds the mass together while it hardens, and acts as a core when the concrete has set. For this reason they occasionally inserted pyramidal blocks of stone, point foremost, into the soft concrete, so that the stone blocks held the mass together, and, after the concrete had set, the bases of the pyramids formed a pattern on the surface which became known as *opus reticulatum*. Alberti seems to have been unaware of the constructional purpose which underlay this decorative effect, and it is characteristic that he carved a stone surface to represent this network, because he was aiming at a visual effect which had nothing in common with the aims of the original Roman inventors of the technique. Nevertheless, he would have justified his action on the grounds that the visual effect was 'antique'. It is clear also from the cornice at the top of the building that he had specific Roman prototypes in mind. This cornice presented him with a very great difficulty. Michelozzo's immense overhang could be regarded as being proportioned to the whole height of the building, and not merely to the top storey. Alberti, however, was limited by the fact that each of the lower storeys had a complete entablature proportioned to the pilasters carrying it, and it was therefore necessary that the top storey should have a cornice proportioned to the topmost order. This, however, would have been totally inadequate for the practical purpose of providing shade during the heat of the day. Alberti therefore designed the highest possible cornice consistent with the size of the topmost order, but he then gave it a very strongly emphasized overhang and supported the projecting parts by a series of classical corbels inserted into the frieze. In this way one is entitled, when looking at the building from street level, to read the cornice simultaneously as a part of the top storey and also as a part of the building as a whole. The device adopted was, like his use of the orders, copied from the Colosseum, so that, in what is probably his first work, Alberti's whole attitude to classical antiquity is already clearly visible, as is his tendency to regard Roman architecture as the norm for modern architecture.

In spite of Alberti's great authority, both as an architect and as a writer, the Palazzo Rucellai had few successors, and most Florentine architects of the fifteenth and sixteenth centuries evolved a freer type

[39, 40, 42] which can be seen in various forms in several other of the great palaces such as the Pitti, the Pazzi-Quaratesi, and the vast Palazzo Strozzi, built right at the end of the century. The Palazzo Pitti presents many problems. As we now see it, it is mostly of the sixteenth and seventeenth centuries, but we know from paintings and early records that it was intended from the beginning to be gigantic in scale, if not quite so huge as it now is. It consisted originally of seven bays – the central seven of the present façade – and seems to have been begun for Luca Pitti after the middle of the century. Luca Fancelli, who had been Alberti's assistant, was certainly concerned in the work, but the design has been attributed both to Brunelleschi and to Alberti. Its conception is so grandiose that an attribution to Brunelleschi is understandable; but not one of the fifteenth-century sources records it as his work, and an early sixteenth-century source makes it seem highly probable that it was not begun until 1458, twelve years after Brunelleschi's death. Luca Pitti, who thought of himself as Cosimo de' Medici's great rival, was a vain

39 Florence, Palazzo Pitti. Street façade. Central part begun 1458 by an unknown architect

and rather silly old man, and there can be little doubt that he intended to build a palace that would make the Palazzo Medici look insignificant. It may be, therefore, that the model made for Cosimo by Brunelleschi, and rejected as too magnificent, underlies the design of the Palazzo Pitti. An attribution to Alberti seems highly improbable, for two reasons. In the first place, the grandeur of the palace owes nothing to any direct imitation of a Roman prototype. Indirectly, it can be argued that the sheer scale of the building – the storeys are about 40 feet high – derives from a real understanding of Roman architecture, yet this would seem to be almost conclusive evidence against Alberti's authorship, since even the enormous barrel-vault of S. Andrea at Mantua lacks the stark simplicity of the Palazzo Pitti, and there is no other work by him which demonstrates so confident a handling of large empty spaces.

Whoever designed the original Palazzo Pitti seems not to have built anything else, since all the other late fifteenth- and early sixteenth-century Florentine palaces derive more or less directly from a prototype such as the Palazzo Medici, and few of them make any

40 Florence, Palazzo Pazzi-Quaratesi, 1462/70

41 Florence, Palazzo Gondi.
Begun *c.* 1490 by Giuliano da Sangallo

advance on it. The Palazzo Pazzi-Quaratesi and the Palazzo Gondi [40, 41] may be taken as typical of the late fifteenth-century trend, discernible in all the arts, towards smoothness and prettiness and away from the rugged and heroic style of Masaccio, Donatello, and Brunelleschi. The Palazzo Pazzi-Quaratesi has a traditional association with the name of Brunelleschi; and the rustication of the ground floor, and the design of the building as a whole, reflects his style in very general terms. On the other hand, much of the work seems to date from 1462/70, while the decorative sculpture can be associated with Giuliano and Benedetto da Maiano. This decoration is typical of the late fifteenth century in its freedom and charm, but it could not under any circumstances be dated before 1450.

The Palazzo Gondi was begun about 1490 and was inhabited in 1498. It is the work of the most important of all Brunelleschi's later followers, Giuliano da Sangallo, the eldest member of the most important Florentine architectural dynasty at the end of the fifteenth

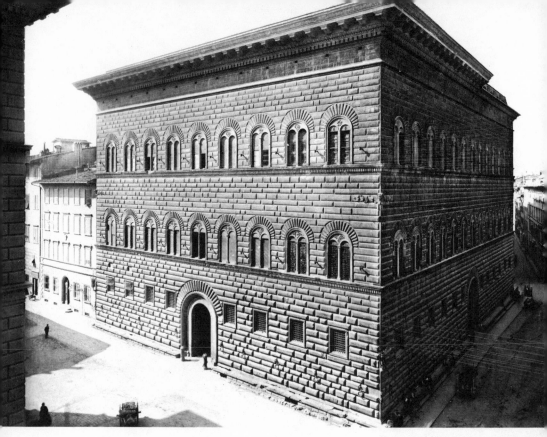

42 Florence, Palazzo Strozzi. Begun 1489

century. Giuliano was born about 1443 and died in 1516, so that he was too young to have had much direct contact with the Brunelleschi and Michelozzo generation. Nevertheless, the Palazzo Gondi is very close indeed to the Palazzo Medici and also to the other great descendant of the Palazzo Medici, the Palazzo Strozzi. The Palazzo Gondi is smaller and simpler than the Medici, but its most interesting architectural feature is the transformation of the rustication on the ground floor of the Palazzo Medici from huge rough-hewn lumps of masonry into evenly spaced rounded blocks of more or less the same size. This tendency to smooth out the roughness is further accentuated by the surface patterns introduced on the first floor in the shape of little crosses between the windows, or the pattern made by the voussoirs of the entrances on the ground floor.

80

The Palazzo Strozzi deserves separate mention, if only on account of its sheer size. Once more it is dependent on the Palazzo Medici for almost all its architectural merits. It is very much larger and has rustication, of the same rounded type as that in the Palazzo Gondi, running up the whole height of the façade, but it is only in such very minor details that it differs from the Palazzo Medici. It was begun in 1489, and the grand cornice was designed by Il Cronaca before 1504, although the palace as a whole was probably not finished until 1536. The original wooden model is still preserved there, and there is a document of payment to Giuliano da Sangallo for making it. Nevertheless, it is generally believed that Giuliano was paid only for executing the model, not for designing it; and it may be that the original design should be attributed to Benedetto da Maiano.

The great Florentine palaces provided models for most of the rest of Italy, and almost every Italian town can show several examples of the type of comfortable, large house which, somewhat grandiloquently, is referred to in Italian as a 'palace'. There are a few, dating from the fifteenth century, outside Florence which made advances in one way or another on the type as established in Florence; and the most famous of these are in Pienza, Rome, and Urbino.

When the humanist Æneas Silvius Piccolomini became Pope Pius II in 1458 he began to rebuild his native village, renaming it Pienza after himself. It is a small town, almost exactly half-way between Siena and Perugia, and since its brief moment of glory in the fifteenth century has hardly changed at all; but it occupies an important place in the history of town planning. Pius decided to elevate his village to the status of a city, and because of this he began to build not only a cathedral and a bishop's palace, but also a large palace for himself and his family, and a small town hall. Since he knew well enough that most of the work would have to be completed within his own lifetime, he set about it very early in his pontificate, and, between 1459 and his death in 1464, he had achieved a remarkable piece of town planning. The design was supervised by himself and executed by the Florentine architect Bernardo Rossellino, who had worked for Alberti on the Palazzo Rucellai. Pius was a rather unusual pope and has left us a long and extremely candid autobiography in which several pages[10] are devoted to his activities in Pienza and to the type of building that he wanted to create. First, and far the most important,

81

[43] is the fact that the centre of the town was consciously planned as a single unit based on the cathedral. The layout shows that the cathedral itself lies on the main axis of a piazza, the sides of which converge towards the town hall at the north end. The east and west sides of the piazza are occupied by Pius's own family palace and the bishop's palace, while the south side, apart from the cathedral, slopes very sharply downwards. The cathedral itself is extremely unusual since it is based on an Austrian church which Pius had admired on one of his extensive journeys, journeys which had taken him as far afield as Scotland. He was obviously prepared to impose an architectural type, and this is confirmed by the fact that he left strict instructions that no changes of any kind were ever to be introduced into the structure or decoration of the cathedral.[11] The palace also has new features. In the first place, it is deliberately sited so that it is related to the cathedral, and, secondly, the garden front looks out southwards to a magnificent view towards Monte Amiata. Perhaps it is not surprising that the palace is an almost literal copy of Alberti's Palazzo Rucellai, since Bernardo Rossellino was responsible for building it, but, as Pius had shown elsewhere that he was prepared to impose his architectural preferences, it is worth noting that for his own palace he adopted the strictly symmetrical and classical principles of his fellow humanist, Alberti. There is, however, one exception to this which was due to Pius himself. The south side of the palace consists of three open porticoes, one above the other, looking out across the garden to the distant view of the mountains; and we know that Pius caused these porticoes to be built simply for the sake of the view. Thus, the little city of Pienza contains one of the first pieces of regular town planning since Roman days – apart from one or two medieval examples based on existing Roman market places and similar features – and it seems also to contain the first palace in which the view across an extensive landscape is an important feature in the design. It is often said that Petrarch was the first modern man to climb a mountain for the sake of the view, and it seems that Pius was the first modern to spend money on a building which should provide a view.

According to Pius's own account, Bernardo Rossellino exceeded his estimates. He had spent more than 50,000 ducats (his original estimate was 18,000), and was not unnaturally apprehensive when the Pope sent for him. The autobiography continues: 'When he arrived after a few days in some apprehension since he knew that many

82

charges had been brought against him, Pius said, "You did well, Bernardo, in lying to us about expense involved in the work. If you had told the truth you could never have induced us to spend so much money and neither this splendid palace, nor this church, the finest in all Italy, would now be standing. Your deceit has built these glorious structures which are praised by all except the few that are consumed by envy. We thank you and think you deserve a special honour among all the architects of our time" and he ordered full pay to be given him and, in addition, a present of 100 ducats and a scarlet robe.... Bernardo, when he heard the Pope's words, burst into tears of joy.'

Pius's predecessor, Nicholas V, who died in 1455, had employed Alberti as his consultant on a number of schemes in Rome itself, of which the most important was a project for extensive alterations to St Peter's, which later had a profound effect upon the building as we know it today. Rather surprisingly, Rome was of little importance, either politically or artistically, in the first half of the fifteenth century, largely owing to the absence of the popes. Nicholas and Alberti attempted to do something about the state of the city, but with comparatively little success, and there are only two secular buildings of any real importance which have come down to us from the

43 Pienza, town plan by Pius II. Begun 1458

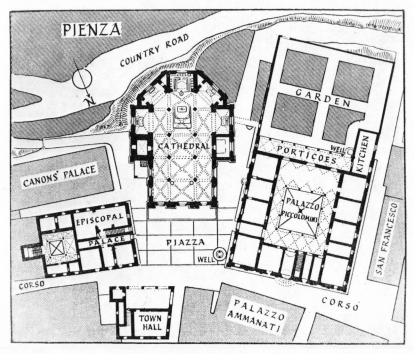

44 Rome,
Palazzo Venezia.
Court, 1467/71

45 Rome, Palazzo
della Cancelleria.
Court, 1486–96

fifteenth century: the palace known as the Palazzo della Cancelleria
[44] and the Palazzo Venezia. In both cases, the influence of Alberti is
very clearly marked, though it is extremely unlikely that he had a
hand in either. The unfinished court of the Palazzo Venezia dates from
1467/71 and is the first important Roman secular building for a very
long time. Although Alberti did not design it, it offers a solution to
the problem of the angles in a courtyard. The problem had, as we
have seen, arisen in buildings like the Palazzo Medici in Florence, but
the Roman solution is characteristic of Alberti in its derivation from

84

a classical prototype, which was either the Colosseum or the ancient Theatre of Marcellus, across the street from the Palazzo Venezia. The court differs from that of the Palazzo Medici, since it is not a series of arches carried on single columns but a series of arches carried on solid piers. The piers have half-columns set on high bases, used as a decorative rather than a structural element as in both the Roman prototypes. From the point of view of architectural design this has the great advantage over the Florentine type that the angles have an appearance of greater solidity, caused by the L-shape of the piers;

together with a better spacing of the columns, since their proportions can be adjusted to suit the bases below them. Very probably this idea was first worked out by Alberti, inspired by the Colosseum, and used by him in the Benediction Loggia of Old St Peter's which is known to us from drawings. These drawings show that the Benediction Loggia was the link between the Colosseum and the Palazzo Venezia; and Alberti must therefore be given the credit for this particular innovation.

[45, 46]   The second important building, the Palazzo della Cancelleria, is an enormous palace begun for Cardinal Riario but subsequently taken over as the Papal Chancery, from which it derives its name. The Palazzo della Cancelleria is one of the greatest mysteries of Italian architecture. It seems certain that it was designed and largely built between 1486 and 1496. Like the Palazzo Pitti in Florence, it is enormous in scale and shows the influence of Alberti, although it cannot possibly be by him since he died long before it was begun. It used to be attributed to Bramante, presumably because it is so fine a building, but Bramante is not known to have arrived in Rome before the winter of 1499–1500, and there is no doubt that the decisive features of the Palazzo della Cancelleria were fixed well before then. The enormously long façade consists of a high podium with two storeys above, both of which have pilaster facings. It is obvious at a glance

[38]   that the type is very similar to the Palazzo Rucellai, but the Palazzo della Cancelleria is more subtle in its proportions, and, for this reason, is far in advance of Rossellino's rather feeble copy at Pienza. In the first place, the horizontal division into three parts is made simpler and clearer than the same division in the Palazzo Rucellai by the omission of the pilasters on the ground floor. The rustication and the comparatively small windows of the ground floor are thus made to form a large and imposing base for the two upper storeys, both of which are also rusticated. The upper storeys are, however, differently treated. The *piano nobile* has grander windows, and the attic storey two windows in each bay, instead of the single large one on the floor below. The great mass of wall is broken up both vertically and horizontally by projections at the ends of the façade, although it must be admitted that these projections are really too shallow to be fully effective. The horizontal articulation is both more effective and more subtle. In the Palazzo Rucellai Alberti had established a very simple pattern of identical window bays separated by single pilasters, each

86

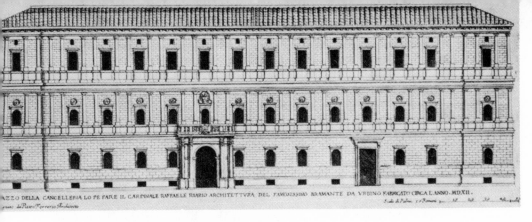

AZZO DELLA CANCELLERIA LO FE FARE IL CARDINALE RAFFAELE RIARIO ARCHITETTVRA DEL FAMOSISSIMO BRAMANTE DA VRBINO FABRICATO CIRCA L ANNO. MDXII .

grave di Pietro Ferrerio Architetto

46 Rome, Palazzo della Cancelleria. Elevation

of which stood on the cornice of the pilaster below it, the cornice thus serving as sill for the windows and base for the pilasters. The Palazzo della Cancelleria has a more complex rhythm, consisting of a pair of pilasters with a narrow, windowless bay between them, followed by a wider bay containing the window, so that in place of the A A B A A B rhythm of the Palazzo Rucellai we now have A B A B A B. Both the sills of the window and the bases of the pilasters are now separate, and kept distinct from the cornice of the order below. The introduction of wide and narrow bays leads also to a new kind of proportion. In place of the simple 1 : 2, or 2 : 3 proportions of the earlier palaces, the Cancelleria makes extensive use of the irrational proportion known as the Golden Section. Thus, for example, the width of an entire four-pilaster unit is to its height as the height of one of the main windows is to its width, and the same proportion rules the widths of the narrower and the wider bays. From this alone it is clear that the architect of the Cancelleria was a man deeply versed in Alberti's theory as well as his practice, and one capable of advancing the art of architecture by a considerable degree.

The court façade is in some ways even closer to the Palazzo Rucellai, because it is derived directly from the Colosseum type of elevation with columns on the lower floors and pilasters on the top storey. The two lower storeys have rather wide arches supported on columns, reminiscent of the Foundling Hospital, but the top storey has a variation on the main façade at the same level, with single pilasters in place of pairs, making the internal rhythm A A A. It is, however, on the lower storeys that we find an important difference

87

in the treatment of the angles, distinct both from the Palazzo Medici type and from that used in the Palazzo Venezia court. As in the earlier forms, the arches are carried on single columns, but the difficulty of the angle is resolved by the use of an L-shaped pier, as in the Palazzo Venezia. All these subtleties have led to the belief that, if anywhere, it was in this part of the palace that Bramante may have been concerned. This opinion is strengthened rather than weakened by the fact that Bramante came originally from Urbino – and it is there that we find the first datable example of this solution to the angle problem.

[47–50]   The Palazzo Ducale at Urbino is the third of these great non-Florentine buildings of the second half of the fifteenth century. It was built mainly during the 1460s for the greatest soldier of the age, Federigo, Duke of Urbino, whose small court was probably the most civilized centre in the whole of Europe.

The palace at Urbino also presents considerable problems, both of attribution and dating, but on the whole it seems most likely that the important parts were built by the rather mysterious Dalmatian architect, Luciano Laurana. We know very little about Laurana and nothing about his early training, but we do know that he was in Urbino by 1465/6, and he is named as the Architect-in-Chief of the palace in a document of 1468. He died at Pesaro in 1479. It seems most likely that the courtyard of the palace, which is its chief glory, can be dated between 1465 and 1479 and it is therefore reasonable to assume that both it and the main entrance façade are the work of Laurana. There were, however, other artists at work in Urbino and the palace was certainly begun before Laurana appeared on the scene. It was probably completed by the Sienese Francesco di Giorgio, and there is still room for debate about the exact demarcations between Laurana and Francesco in some of the interior decoration. Further-more, we know that the Duke, who was Commander-in-Chief of the Papal Forces and a man who had risen from very humble begin-nings, was on friendly terms with almost all the major artists of the day, and Piero della Francesca, Mantegna, and Alberti were all welcome visitors at Urbino. It was there, in 1444, that Bramante was born and there, thirty-nine years later, Raphael was also born. Attempts have been made to give the credit for the extraordinary perfection of the proportions, both of the court and the main façade of the palace, to Piero della Francesca; but there seems no reason to

88

doubt the enthusiastic terms in which Federigo speaks of Luciano Laurana in the document of 1468 which refers to him as the Architect-in-Chief.[12]

The palace at Urbino is situated on the very top of a mountain with the ground falling steeply away from it on every side except that of the main entrance, which faces the piazza and cathedral. As with the palace at Pienza, the superb view was taken into account, and on the steepest side two high, round towers were built with three round-headed openings between them forming a loggia on each of the three storeys looking out across the mountains. This triumphal arch type of design can be connected with the triumphal arch built in Naples for Alfonso of Aragon and it is possible that Laurana began his career working there. The court and the main entrance façade are, however, the most important parts of the palace as it exists, although the interior with large, bare rooms, elaborately carved fireplaces, and doorways with perhaps the finest existing intarsia work, is one of the most beautiful that has come down to us. The palace is now the National Gallery of the Marches and contains a collection of paintings worthy of its setting.

The façade of the palace seen from the main piazza of the town is [47] at first sight, like so many Italian buildings, very disappointing. It is riddled with the small holes intended for the scaffolding poles and is obviously unfinished, with some of the major windows walled up and some of the doorways much reduced in size. Nevertheless, it well repays a closer study. The first thing clearly visible is that the main entrance façade, which has three doorways and four main windows, is entirely different, both in size and in disposition of the windows, from the other main front of the palace, where the windows are all round-headed and some of them are of the two-light form familiar from much earlier Florentine palaces. We know that part of the palace was begun in 1447 and it is reasonable, therefore, to assume that these round-headed, rather Florentine windows date from then. The main façade of the palace is exceedingly skilfully arranged as a rusticated basement storey which has pilasters at the angles and has three large square-headed entrance doorways with smaller square-headed windows between them. Above this, on the *piano nobile*, there are four windows, similar in type to the doorways, flanked by pilasters and with strongly modelled straight entablatures acting as hood mouldings for the windows. Above this again, the architect must

89

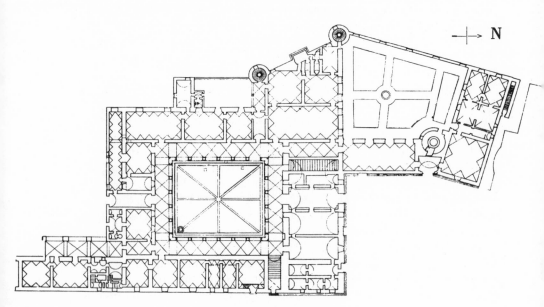

URBINO, PALAZZO DUCALE
by Laurana (?),
designed before 1468

47 Façade

48 Plan

49 Court

50 Door

have planned at least one attic storey, but in the present state of the façade we can only guess what it might have looked like.[13] The very unusual disposition of the four main windows above three large doorways, so that the rhythm is a kind of zigzag with the void of the window set above the rusticated bays and the void of the doorway set between the two windows, is an entirely different idea of a façade from that which would have been held by any Florentine architect of the mid fifteenth century. At the same time, the actual shapes of the rectangular openings differ from those normal in Florence, and once more we must assume that the architect was Luciano Laurana and that the façade of the palace remained incomplete when he left Urbino.

[49]   If we go through the last of the three doorways, we find ourselves in the courtyard of the palace. Here again, the elements are Florentine in type and clearly refer to such great examples as the Palazzo Medici, yet these same elements are handled with a skill and sophistication far in advance of that possessed by any native Florentine of the 1460s and 1470s. A comparison of the court with that of the Palazzo Medici shows that in both cases the ground floor consists of an open cloister with cross vaults carried on columns. Immediately above it the *piano nobile* is closed in and has windows corresponding to the arches on the ground floor. It is here that the superiority of the court at Urbino is manifested. In the first place, the weakness of the Palazzo Medici court is largely due to the difficulty of turning the two arches at right angles on a single column in each of the corners. A solution to this difficulty had already been found, as we have seen, in the courtyard of [44]   the Palazzo Venezia in Rome, which was very probably inspired by Alberti and which must date from about the same time as the work at Urbino. Laurana has made an L-shaped pier at the angles, each faced with a half-column carrying the ground-floor arches. The pier is faced by pilasters which meet at the angle, and which carry an entablature bearing a Latin inscription praising the virtues of Duke Federigo.[14] This pilaster and entablature system running above the arches is obviously inspired by Brunelleschi's Foundling Hospital, so that Laurana has adapted Brunelleschi's invention in a way which Brunelleschi's fellow Florentines had not worked out for themselves. More important, the arrangement of the angles allows each of the windows on the *piano nobile* to be centred over the arches below them without crowding together at the angles and with sufficient space

92

round them to allow for a pilaster order corresponding to the columns on the ground floor. We now have the two strong horizontals of the upper and lower entablature with the bays of both storeys clearly defined by a consistent use of pilasters and columns. The actual proportion of the window openings to the space between the framing pilasters is a particularly good example of the extreme delicacy of perception of this architect; by comparison Michelozzo's courtyard appears clumsy and insensitive. There can be little doubt that the architect of the court at Urbino was the same as the designer of the main façade, and equally there can be no doubt that he was not a Florentine, although he was very well informed on all the most recent work in Florence, Rome, and Naples. Since we know that Laurana was Federigo's Architect-in-Chief in 1468, it may be assumed that he was the genius who left behind this one perfect work, which in turn was to inspire the greatest architect of the next generation, Bramante.

One other architect of great ability also worked on the palace at Urbino – the Sienese painter and architect Francesco di Giorgio. It seems, however, most likely that he was principally concerned with the decoration of some of the rooms since the one certain architectural work by him, the small church near Cortona which dates from the [61] end of the century, is by no means of the same quality as the palace at Urbino where San Bernardino has also been attributed to him.

The design of the typical Venetian palace is fundamentally different from that of all other Italian palaces and the stylistic development of Venetian architecture is also considerably slower. As we have seen, the normal type of palace represented by the Florentine examples was conditioned by a number of social, economic, and climatic factors. The Venetian type was subject to the same influences, but the factors were themselves different. In the first place, because of the shortage of land, almost every major palace in Venice is built to a large extent on piles driven into the water, which means that there is no dry land for a central open court. The economic and political stability of Venice also made it less necessary to fortify the palaces and there was thus no need for a central light well. The Venetian palace therefore tends to be a single block, and the style in which it was built was profoundly modified by the facts of Venetian trade. During the Middle Ages the Venetians traded extensively in the Eastern

Mediterranean and particularly with the Eastern Roman Empire as it existed until Constantinople fell to the Turks in 1453. There was thus a profound influence from Byzantine art, which was a living force in Venice generations after it had died in the rest of Italy. Trade with northern Europe also helped to introduce northern Gothic ideas.

The two great buildings symbolizing the power and the wealth of the Republic were the Basilica of St Mark and the Doges' Palace. The Basilica of St Mark dates back to 829 but was rebuilt in 1063 and consecrated in 1094. A good deal of the façade dates from the early fifteenth century. The Doges' Palace was built in the fourteenth century but the side facing the piazza – parallel, that is, to the façade of St Mark's – dates from about 1424–42. These two buildings, and in [51] particular the Doges' Palace, provide the permanent exemplars for Venetian architecture, as may be seen from an example like the [52] Ca' d'Oro of 1427/36 or the Palazzo Pisani of the middle of the fifteenth century. In these and in later examples of the same type of palace, the influence of the Doges' Palace is most evident in the shape and size of the windows on the first floor. In the Ca' d'Oro we see once more the strange but highly successful device of a double arcade with the wide openings on the ground floor and the narrow ones immediately above it, but the Ca' d'Oro, unlike the Doges' Palace,

51 Venice, the Doges' Palace. 14th and 15th century

52 Venice, Ca' d'Oro.
1427/36

stands on and partly in the Grand Canal. Not only does this mean that
the palace has no central court but it also means that the ground floor
is virtually uninhabitable. The typical Venetian palace, therefore,
has a large opening at water-level with a flight of stairs running out
of an entrance hall and a number of store-rooms occupying the rest
of the ground floor just above the water-level. The *piano nobile* is thus
even more important in Venetian palaces than in any other Italian
examples. This leads to a further characteristic of Venetian palace
design, namely the tendency to divide the façade into three vertical
elements. The main room on the first floor, known as the *Gran Salone*,
occupies the whole of the centre of the façade, and the smaller rooms
on either side of it are expressed externally by smaller windows. This,
in turn, means that the windows of the *Gran Salone* must be as large
as possible since the great room inside can be lit only from the back and
the front, there being no possibility of side lighting and no internal
court. Hence the most characteristic feature of all Venetian palaces,

53 Venice, Palazzo Corner-Spinelli. Begun c. 1480

the great mass of window openings in the centre of the façade. Venetian conservatism was such that this basic type of design lasted virtually unchanged from the early fifteenth to the eighteenth century and the only important modifications, introduced gradually in the course of the fifteenth and sixteenth centuries, all lay in the direction of systematizing the façade into a symmetrical disposition with more or less regular openings. Most of the great fifteenth- and early sixteenth-century palaces were designed by one or other of the Lombardi, or by their relation, Mauro Codussi, and their work may be seen in such

54 Venice, Palazzo Vendramin-Calergi. Begun *c.* 1500–9

palaces as the Corner-Spinelli, begun about 1480 and the Palazzo [53, 54]
Vendramin-Calergi, begun about 1500 and finished in 1509. In both
cases the central massing of the windows has been retained, but the
windows in the bays at either side have been symmetrically disposed
and are made the same size and shape as those in the centre. In the
Corner-Spinelli, the rhythm is A B B A and in the Vendramin-Calergi
it is A B B B A, but in the latter example the classical elements are
handled with a little more assurance and skill, as for example in the
arrangement of the attached columns. Here, the traditional disposition

97

of the windows is stressed by the fact that the side bays have a pair of columns, a window, and another pair of columns, whereas the three main windows of the *Gran Salone* are separated only by single columns. Nevertheless, when one considers what was happening in the rest of Italy by 1509, the Palazzo Vendramin-Calergi must be regarded as essentially old fashioned, and it was not until about 1537 when Jacopo Sansovino, a Florentine refugee in Venice, began his magnificent palace for the Cornaro family, that High Renaissance forms can be said to have arrived there.

One other architectural form peculiar to Venice should be mentioned in passing – the type of charitable foundation known as a *Scuola*. These were religious confraternities, usually of men engaged in the same occupation, who, under the patronage of a particular saint, banded themselves together to carry out charitable and educational work. The buildings were thus sometimes partly hospitals or schools, but at the same time they served as a meeting–place for the members. The most famous architecturally are probably the Scuola di S. Marco, and the Scuola di S. Rocco, which was not built until 1517–60, but nevertheless shows the extreme conservatism of Venetian architects, coupled with the permanent influence of St Mark's on all ecclesiastical buildings in Venice.

The influence of St Mark's conditioned almost all churches in Venice and Venetian territory for many years to come. It can be seen in such buildings as Sta Maria de' Miracoli or S. Zaccaria, both of which date from the second half of the fifteenth century and are once more the works of Mauro Codussi and the Lombardi family. Only two Venetian churches of this period call for special mention: [55] S. Michele in Isola, which was Codussi's first work in Venice, begun in 1469 and completed about 1479, and the much later S. Salvatore. It is tempting to assert that S. Michele in Isola is Codussi's finest work simply because it shows less of the Venetian passion for decoration than any other of his buildings. It was built on the small island which serves as the cemetery of Venice and is therefore a mortuary chapel rather than a parish church. Perhaps for this reason the architecture has a simplicity and severity far more akin to the early work of Alberti than to later fifteenth-century Venetian architecture. The similarities between S. Michele and Alberti's Tempio Malatestiano can hardly be coincidental and must be the source of the classic impulse in Venice at that date.

98

55 Venice, S. Michele in Isola. 1469–*c.* 1479 by Codussi

[56]   The second church, S. Salvatore, was built between 1507 and 1534 and is principally of interest for the way in which it evolves the Latin cross type of church into a new form derived directly from St Mark's since it consists of a long nave made up of three interlocked central plans, each of which is a large dome surrounded by four smaller domes – thus combining the type of St Mark's with that evolved in Milan by Filarete and Leonardo (see below, pp. 107–12). The Latin cross is obtained by the addition of transepts and apses. The plan seems to be due to Giorgio Spavento, but the work was carried out by one of the Lombardi and even by Jacopo Sansovino.

The north of Italy provides several examples of the mixed style which resulted from an application of the classical principles of Tuscan architects to the decorative traditions common in the north.

[57]   One of the most important of these buildings is the Colleone Chapel at Bergamo by the famous and much-employed Giovanni Antonio Amadeo, who was later to collaborate with Bramante in Milan. The Colleone Chapel was built in the first half of the 1470s and shows close similarities to Filarete's work in that it has a high, octagonal, drum with a dome and lantern which derive ultimately from Florence Cathedral. Nevertheless, the façade as a whole shows that the decorative elements could always triumph over the mathematical principles of the Tuscan architects, even though Amadeo probably

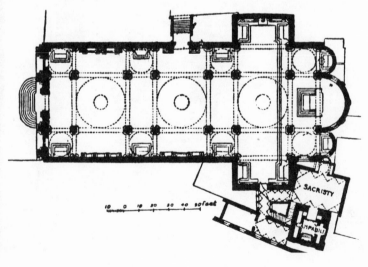

56 Venice,
S. Salvatore. Plan by
Giorgio Spavento,
c. 1507

57 Bergamo, Cappella Colleone by Amadeo, early 1470s

thought of himself as a classical architect. A very much more success-ful, though much later, building is Como Cathedral, dating from the end of the century. Less successful, though more famous, is the great Carthusian monastery, the Certosa at Pavia which was designed about 1481, but took nearly 150 years to complete. Amadeo probably had a share in the design, but most of the major Milanese architects, painters, and sculptors were employed on it. Much of the sculpture on the façade is extremely fine as sculpture, but the general effect is best described as cluttered. In fact, the main lines of the design are simple, but they are so overlaid with coloured incrustations and decorative sculpture that the total effect is one of half-digested classicism.

The only other important churches built in Italy in the last years of the fifteenth century were by Tuscan architects developing the principles laid down by Brunelleschi. These include Sta Maria delle Carceri, at Prato, by Giuliano da Sangallo, and Sta Maria del Calcinaio, near Cortona, by Francesco di Giorgio. Both these resemble the experiments with centrally planned churches being carried out in Milan by Leonardo and Bramante, and we know that Francesco di Giorgio was personally acquainted with Leonardo and wrote a treatise on architecture.

Giuliano da Sangallo was the eldest of the three major architects in the family. He was born probably in 1443 and died in 1516. His brother, known as Antonio the Elder, was born in 1455 and their nephew, Antonio the Younger, was born in 1485. Giuliano began life as a woodworker and was brought up in the tradition established by Brunelleschi (who died when Giuliano was a child of about three). His most important works are the church at Prato, the Palazzo Gondi in Florence, and the Sacristy which he added to Brunelleschi's church of Sto Spirito. His career culminated in his official appointment to succeed Bramante as the Head of the Works at St Peter's, but he was by then (1514–15) obviously incapable of so enormous an undertaking and he retired to Florence, where he died in 1516. His two ecclesiastical works show very clearly his attachment to the Brunelleschian tradition, since the Sacristy at Sto Spirito resembles the Baptistry of Florence with the detailing entirely in Brunelleschi's manner. The church of Sta Maria delle Carceri at Prato was begun in 1485 and was left in its present incomplete state in 1506. It is a pure Greek cross and derives, therefore, from the Brunelleschian tradition of centrally

[58–61]

PRATO, STA MARIA DELLE CARCERI
by Giuliano da Sangallo, begun 1485

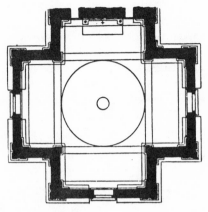

58 Plan

59 Section

60 Interior

planned churches but also, and more immediately, from Alberti's S. Sebastiano at Mantua, a quarter of a century earlier. The interior shows a ribbed dome supported on pendentives, exactly like Brunelleschi's Pazzi Chapel or Old Sacristy; but the exterior, where there was no immediate Brunelleschian prototype to borrow from, is much weaker with a very awkwardly proportioned double order. Nevertheless, both in Giuliano's church and in Francesco di Giorgio's similar and contemporary Sta Maria del Calcinaio, we see the culmination of the Early Renaissance ideals of classical lightness and purity. The next stage was to be reached by Bramante.

61 Cortona, Sta Maria del Calcinaio, interior. Late 15th century, by Francesco di Giorgio

CHAPTER FIVE

Milan: Filarete, Leonardo, Bramante

The second half of the fifteenth century saw very important developments in Milan. The Sforza family dominated the political scene from 1450, when Francesco Sforza was made Duke of Milan, until 1499, when Lodovico lost the city to Louis XII of France and ended his life in prison. The Sforzas, particularly Lodovico, were great patrons of the arts and the two greatest artists in the world, Leonardo da Vinci and Bramante, both worked for him for nearly twenty years. At the time of Francesco Sforza's accession to the dukedom, the Florentines were still supreme in all the arts and a strong Tuscan influence was soon overlaid on the native Lombard tradition, largely because Francesco Sforza was politically allied to the Florence of Cosimo de' Medici. A number of Florentine artists, including Brunelleschi himself, worked in Milan for varying periods, but the three most influential were Michelozzo, Filarete, and Leonardo da Vinci. So far as we know, Michelozzo designed two important buildings in Milan: a palace belonging to the Medici family, and a large chapel built by the Florentine family of Portinari. The Portinari Chapel is part of the Basilica of S. Eustorgio but can almost rank as a separate [62] building; it is attributed to Michelozzo, but it is by no means certain that the design is entirely his or that it was executed by the Milanese craftsmen precisely as he intended. The Milanese tradition, with its love of colour and decoration, was obviously opposed to the simpler and more austere forms which Michelozzo had learned from Brunelleschi; and the history of a good deal of Milanese architecture of the late fifteenth and early sixteenth centuries is the history of a series of compromises between a pure classical style and the traditions and preferences of local patrons and craftsmen. The Portinari Chapel is basically a Brunelleschian type of design, square in plan, with a dome over it supported on pendentives, but it also has four small towers at each corner curiously like minarets, which are typical of Lombard decorative ideas. This type of centrally planned building with towers at the corners was to become characteristic of the late fifteenth-century Lombard interest in the central plan, and the same ideas can

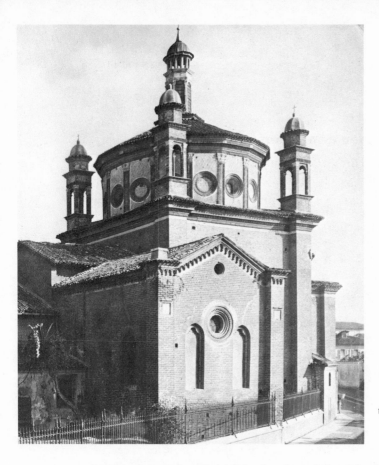

62 Milan,
S. Eustorgio,
the Portinari Chapel.
Early 1460s,
by Michelozzo

be seen in a far more highly developed form in the early projects for the rebuilding of St Peter's in Rome.

The palace which Michelozzo is supposed to have built as the headquarters of the Medici bank in Milan is now known to us only from the main doorway, preserved in the Castello Sforzesco in Milan, and from a drawing of the whole façade in Filarete's treatise on architecture. Both the drawing and the existing doorway show the same combination of Florentine, or Brunelleschian, forms, with Gothic decorative elements such as the pointed windows recorded in Filarete's drawing. Both the Portinari Chapel and the Palazzo Medici date from the early 1460s and are the most important examples of the introduction of Florentine ideas into Milan about the middle of the century.

The next wave of Florentine influence is associated with the name of Filarete. He was a Florentine sculptor whose real name was Antonio Averlino, but who, typically, called himself Filarete, that being approximately Greek for 'lover of virtue'. He was born probably about 1400 and died about 1469, and his earliest surviving major work is the great bronze doors of Old St Peter's, finished in 1445. These doors are among the very few surviving objects trans-ferred to the present Basilica and they clearly show that Filarete hoped to rival the great bronze doors made by Ghiberti for the Baptistry in Florence. They are not, however, very successful; and about two or three years later Filarete left Rome rather hurriedly and apparently under a cloud. Soon after this he arrived in Lombardy where, in 1456, he began the building of the great Milanese hospital which, very greatly altered and rebuilt, survived as the principal one in Milan until very recent years (it is now part of the University of Milan). Before beginning it he visited the hospitals in Florence and Siena, which were then the two great examples of hospital planning. His own building was intended to bring together on one site all the very numerous charitable foundations which were then scattered about in Milan, and it is of architectural importance because the whole vast building was planned as a cross in a square, with the hospital church standing in the very centre of the design, at the junction of the arms of the cross, and itself a centrally planned building. This church, like Michelozzo's Portinari Chapel, also had towers at the angles. Surviving parts of the building show that Filarete, like Michelozzo, attempted to impose classical forms on the Gothic-minded craftsmen and, again like Michelozzo, failed to achieve his object.

More important than his few surviving buildings was the treatise which he wrote, probably between 1461 and 1464. Soon after he completed it he fell out of favour in Milan, and there is a version of the treatise dedicated to Piero de' Medici and dated 1465, which has very numerous illustrations. It is an impassioned plea for a return to the antique style and for the complete abandonment of the 'barbarous modern style' – by which he meant Gothic, still almost unchallenged in North Italy. The work consists of twenty-five books divided in the most extraordinary manner into separate threads of ideas. The first is a perfectly straightforward architectural treatise based on the theories of Alberti, but very muddled and incoherent in expression. The second part of the treatise is an elaborate fairy-tale about an

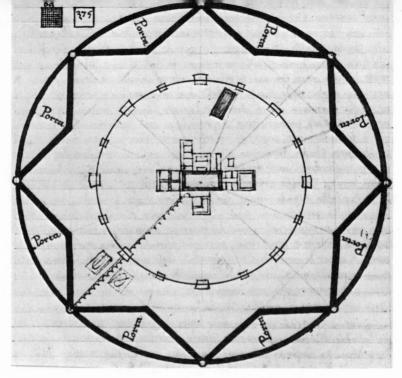

63 Sforzinda, a design for an Ideal City, by Filarete. Before 1464

[*63*]   imaginary city called Sforzinda, named after his Milanese patrons.
There are long descriptions of the city itself, which is very important
as an early example of the star-shaped city plan, and there are also
long descriptions of the individual buildings, together with minute
descriptions of the decorations in the major buildings. It may be
recalled that Pienza, though far less ambitious in its planning than
Sforzinda, was actually being built in the early 1460s. Some of the
books contain the most extraordinary farrago of the astrological
çalculations necessary to secure harmony within the projected city,
followed by common-sense remarks about the desirable relationship
between architect and patron, or the building of fortifications.
Book XI contains a description of the hospital he hoped to build in
Milan, together with some drawings. In the fourteenth book, the
fairy-tale atmosphere is intensified by a description of the Golden
Book, found while digging the foundations of Sforzinda, and which
came from the tomb of someone called King Zogalia. The Golden

108

Book proves to contain descriptions of antique buildings; and it is obvious that, for Filarete at any rate, the remains of antiquity had a semi-magical quality by which they deserved to triumph over the barbarous Gothic. A later generation found Filarete faintly ridiculous and indeed Vasari, writing in the middle of the sixteenth century, describes the treatise rather acidly: 'Although there is some good to be found in it, it is nevertheless very ridiculous, and perhaps the most stupid book that was ever written.' This was the viewpoint of a more rationalistic and more pedantic generation, but there can be little doubt that Filarete's enthusiasm and, above all, his passionate advocacy of the centrally planned form, were of the greatest importance in the development of architectural theory in Milan. Since both Leonardo and Bramante were much occupied with the theory of centrally planned buildings in the 1480s and 1490s, the consequences for Europe as a whole can hardly be over-estimated.

Leonardo da Vinci arrived in Milan most probably in 1482, and remained there until 1499. During these seventeen years he was occupied in making a clay model for the great Sforza Monument, in painting the *Last Supper*, and in profound researches into anatomy and a number of other scientific pursuits. At the same time, probably under the influence of Filarete's treatise and of Bramante, he began to work on a series of centrally planned architectural drawings. It is possible that Leonardo's knowledge of anatomy, which was then incomparably greater than that possessed by anyone else, was what attracted him to the study of architectural drawing. We know that he projected and began to write an elaborate treatise on anatomy in which the whole structure of the human body was explained by means of diagrams based on sections and on drawings of the different stages of dissection, so arranged that the functions of the different parts of the body were clearly manifested. Before this time the professional teaching of anatomy consisted almost exclusively of a few diagrams, which symbolized rather than represented the parts of the body, and of the occasional instruction of medical practitioners by means of a dissection, which was not carried out in order to explore the structure of the human body, but was thought of rather as a means of ratifying the existing diagrams. Leonardo's scientific approach to anatomy is reflected in the numerous architectural drawings of this period,   [64, 65] particularly those contained in the manuscript known as MS. B,

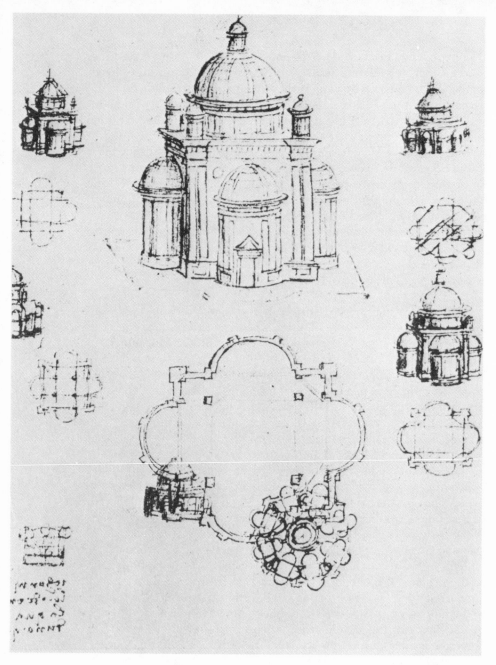

64, 65 Leonardo da Vinci,

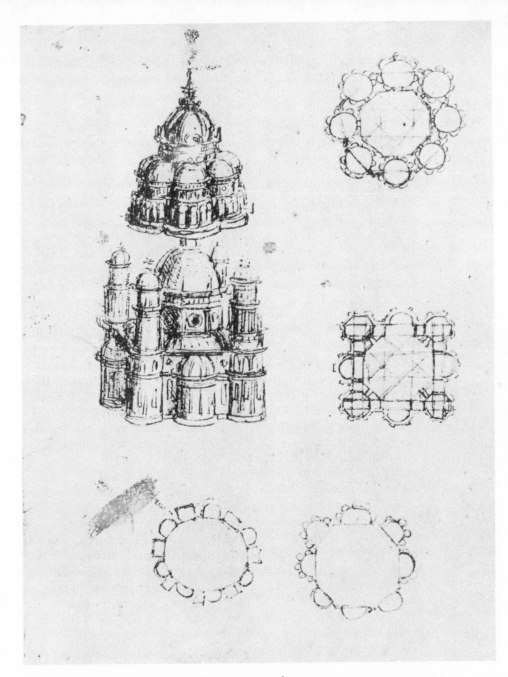

architectural drawings from MS 'B'. *c.* 1489 or later

now in Paris. In this draft of a treatise on architecture Leonardo takes a number of centrally planned forms and evolves more and more complex forms from the first simple shape. Many of these could hardly have been built and are quite obviously exercises in architectural theory, but the importance of these drawings lies in the fact that they are conscious theoretical speculations for which Leonardo evolved a new technique of representation. Most of these drawings present a complex plan and then show the same building in a bird's-eye view (and occasionally in section as well), so that, as with his anatomical drawings, we are given a complete picture of the three-dimensional forms.[15] So far as we know, Leonardo never actually built anything, but there can be no doubt that his drawings and speculations were profoundly influential on Bramante, and, through him, affected the whole current of architectural thought in the sixteenth century. There is even reason to believe that Bramante's early design for St Peter's was much influenced by Leonardo's drawings of centrally planned structures: both men were impressed by the oldest buildings in Milan, above all, by the Early Christian Basilica of S. Lorenzo.

Bramante, who was to become the greatest architect of his generation, was in Milan from at least 1481 until the fall of the city in 1499. His early career is obscure. He was probably born in 1444, not far from Urbino, but nothing whatever is known about him until 1477, when he painted some frescoes in Bergamo of which a few fragments still survive. It seems certain that he was a painter until considerably later than this, since there is an engraving datable in 1481 and inscribed 'in Milan'. This is the earliest evidence of his interest in architecture, but it contains ruined buildings in the highly decorated Lombard Gothic style and it would seem to betray the imagination of a painter rather than an architect. He was presumably brought up in Urbino and there is good reason to believe that he was the pupil of Piero della Francesca and of Mantegna, so that the formative influences on him should have been the noble simplicity of the Palace at Urbino, the harmony of the paintings of Piero, and the passionate interest in classical antiquity of Mantegna. Little of this can be seen in the engraving of 1481, but within the next twenty-five years Bramante was to invent the architectural equivalents of those principles and to express them in a classical vocabulary which was to become the norm for all architecture for centuries to come.

Bramante's earliest known building was the reconstruction of the [66–69] church of Sta Maria presso S. Satiro, a small ninth-century building in Milan. He probably began to work there in the 1470s, although there is no documentary mention of him until 1482. Two things make this small church important for the future. The first is the fact that the east end is constructed as a perspective illusion, showing that Bramante was still deeply influenced by his training as a painter and above all by the architectural ideals of Piero della Francesca. This feeling for architectural space as a series of planes and voids, like those in a painting, rather than as a series of three-dimensional solids, like sculpture, distinguishes Bramante from Brunelleschi and from most of the Florentine architects of his own generation. In fact, the east end of S. Satiro could not be built in the normal manner because of a narrow street running across the end of the building. In order to maintain the ideal spatial effect of choir, nave, and transepts as a unity, Bramante was forced to evolve this ingenious illusion. The decorative character of the coffered vaulting and the forms of the pilasters derive from Piero della Francesca and also from Bramante's study of the surviving Early Christian buildings in Milan itself.

By far the most important of these was the great fifth-century Basilica of S. Lorenzo. Unfortunately, S. Lorenzo was much altered in the sixteenth century and most of the other, once numerous, Early Christian churches in Milan have either disappeared or been profoundly modified. Nevertheless, these fifth- and sixth-century buildings were, for Bramante, the principal evidence of good architectural style and they were undoubtedly the principal source of classic inspiration in his work. This can be proved quite easily at S. Satiro since the small chapel (at left in plate 66) is the original church of S. Satiro dating from the ninth century. Bramante remodelled it, particularly on the exterior, but the plan – a Greek cross in a square inside a circle – is a typical Early Christian design and was adapted by Bramante himself in the Baptistry at S. Satiro (at right in plate 66). What is still more important is that although the plan of the Baptistry is derived directly from Early Christian prototypes, it is also influenced by the Florentine architectural tradition going back to Brunelleschi.[16] This comparatively simple plan also contains the germ of Bramante's original design for the rebuilding of St Peter's in Rome, and this small Milanese church is thus a direct ancestor of many of the churches built in Italy in the sixteenth and seventeenth centuries.

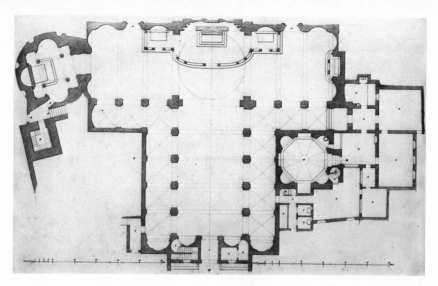

MILAN,
STA MARIA PRESSO S. SATIRO
by Bramante, begun 1470s

66 Plan, with Chapel of S. Satiro on
extreme left and Baptistry on the right

67 Section

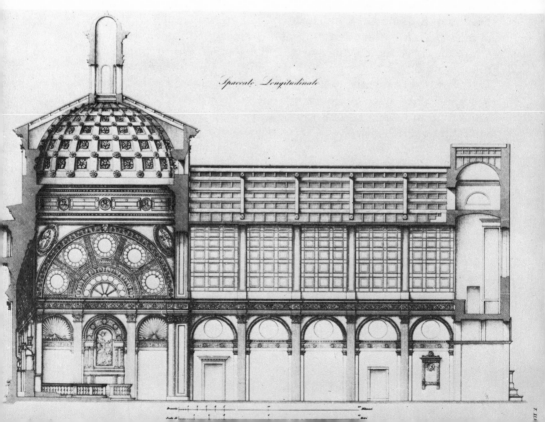

Spaccato Longitudinale

68 Crossing and choir, in false perspective

69 Milan,
Chapel of S. Satiro,
9th century,
remodelled
by Bramante

The Florentine element in Bramante's early style can be accounted for, as we have already seen, by the works of Michelozzo and Filarete, and by the ideas of Filarete and Leonardo da Vinci. The exterior of S. Satiro clearly shows this Florentine influence. Bramante expressed the cross-in-circle plan by developing the building upwards in three main stages. The lowest is cylindrical in shape with deep niches set between pairs of pilasters and alternating with smooth walling. This in itself is reminiscent of Brunelleschi's Sta Maria degli Angeli, but the central plan is emphasized by the fact that the second storey consists of the four arms of the Greek cross rising out of the cylinder. Each of these arms contains a window, and the roofs are gabled. The point at which the gabled roofs meet is made a subsidiary stage, since it becomes a square out of which there rises an octagonal drum with windows alternating between single pilasters. Above this, finally,

[69]

116

there is a small circular lantern. There is a close resemblance to the ideas of Brunelleschi and to such buildings in the Florentine tradition as the Portinari Chapel, but the decorative elements are purely Lombard and the overall effect is still that of an Early-Christian baptistry.

The same general ideas can be seen in a larger work which was left incomplete when Bramante went to Rome: the tribune which he added to the east end of the large church of Sta Maria delle Grazie. [70–72] Work at the Grazie was probably begun in the late 1480s and was continued all through the 1490s. Externally, the building is not very satisfying, since it consists of a long, rather low, nave and aisles, built by another architect in the 1460s with, at the east end, a very large tribune which rises into a great polygonal drum and small lantern. There are apsidal projections on the three free-standing sides, two of which are transepts while the third terminates the choir. The effect, which Bramante undoubtedly sought, is that of an independent, centrally planned building rather loosely attached to a long-nave church. The section and plan show quite clearly the abruptness of the junction. Internally, the effect is more satisfactory, and this is probably due to the fact that much of the decoration represents Bramante's own desires, whereas the exterior was probably executed by local masons, not necessarily under his supervision. The effect of the interior of Sta Maria delle Grazie is one of lightness and clarity, with geometric patterns, such as the painted wheel windows, somewhat reminiscent of the 1481 engraving but nevertheless subordinate to the lucidity of the spatial arrangement. Immediately after he went to Rome, Bramante seems to have turned away from this kind of decoration in an attempt to make his style heavier and grander, more in keeping with the monuments of Roman antiquity. One may perhaps be forgiven for regretting the loss of some of the delicacy and fragility of the forms in Sta Maria delle Grazie and in his other major Milanese work, the three cloisters which he designed for S. Ambrogio and its adjacent monastery. The first of these, the Porta della Canonica, is on one side of the church and consists of a series of round-headed arches supported on columns, with a much larger arch in the centre supported on square piers faced with pilasters. The basic design is something of a combination of the cloister types like Brunelleschi's Foundling Hospital with the famous Roman colonnade outside S Lorenzo in Milan. One small point is of particular interest: the

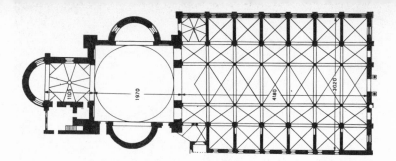

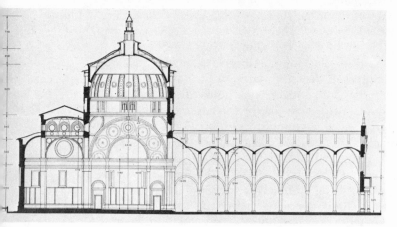

70 Plan

71 Section

72 Interior
of crossing

MILAN, STA MARIA DELLE GRAZIE by Bramante, late 1480s and 1490s

occurrence of several columns with curious excrescences on the shafts. These look rather like tree-trunks with the boughs lopped off, and that is precisely what they are intended to be. Vitruvius, in his account of the beginnings of architecture, asserts that the classical orders took their rise from tree-trunks which were used as vertical supports, and these columns prove, therefore, not only that Bramante retained an eye for picturesque detail, but also that he had been reading Vitruvius during his stay in Milan (the first printed edition is of about 1486, and the first published Italian translation was made by Cesariano, one of Bramante's pupils).

The other two cloisters, known as the Doric and Ionic, were begun by Bramante before he left Milan, but were not finished until much later. They form part of the old monastery of S. Ambrogio, now the Catholic University of Milan. The Doric Cloister is one of his finest and most mature creations. Perhaps the most obvious influence on it

[73]

118

is the court of the Palace at Urbino, which is here combined in the most subtle manner with the Brunelleschian type established at the Foundling Hospital. The vaults of the cloister are supported on dosserets above the columns and the columns themselves are linked by a continuous base. Unlike the court of the Palace at Urbino, the arcade is not strengthened at the angles by a pier but turns on a column, as in the Florentine palace type. Nevertheless, the effect is less unhappy than in the Florentine examples, principally because of the extremely carefully planned relationship between the very large arcades of the ground floor and the much smaller upper storey, which is divided into two small bays over each of the large ground-floor bays. This in turn means that the windows do not come over the centres of the arches, which are marked by small pilasters separating the windows. This particular rhythm owes much to the court at Urbino, but everything in it is dependent upon the extreme precision of the forms and the subtle relationships in proportion. The very flat, sharp mouldings of the pilasters; the blind arcades; the straight-headed windows and the arches of the cloisters; all are as different as possible from the riot of decoration in the engraving of 1481. These are the forms which are usually referred to as his *ultima maniera*, his Roman manner.

73 Milan, S. Ambrogio (now Università Cattolica), Doric Cloister. Bramante, designed 1490s

CHAPTER SIX

Bramante in Rome: St Peter's

After the fall of Lodovico Sforza both Bramante and Leonardo left Milan. Leonardo was later to return and work for the French conquerors but Bramante went straight to Rome, which he reached by the end of 1499, and he spent the rest of his life there. The years between his arrival in the winter of 1499–1500 and the election of Pope Julius II in 1503 are comparatively obscure, but there are at least two works by him of this period, which give a good idea of his mature style. One is the small cloister attached to the church of Sta Maria della Pace, begun about 1500 and completed in 1504, as we learn from an inscription cut in the frieze; the other is the tiny church known as the Tempietto, which stands in the courtyard of the church and monastery of S. Pietro in Montorio. This is dated 1502 on an inscription but building may not have started then.

Bramante was already in his middle fifties when he arrived in Rome so that it was highly unlikely that he would have made any drastic stylistic change; yet we are perfectly justified in regarding the Roman works of the last fourteen years of his life as typifying High Renaissance architecture. Throughout most of the fifteenth century the political importance of Rome had been relatively small, but in the last years of the century, with the pontificate of Sixtus IV and with the decline of the power of Florence after the death in 1492 of Lorenzo de' Medici, Rome once more became politically of great importance and this tendency was greatly strengthened by the pontificate of Julius II (1503–13). Julius was also one of the most enlightened patrons in an age of great patronage and for years on end he had Michelangelo, Raphael, and Bramante all working for him. The artistic importance of Rome at this period was thus very great indeed, since the greatest opportunities were to be found there; yet in the fifteenth century men like Donatello, Alberti, and Brunelleschi had frequently gone there, not in the hope of commissions, but simply to learn from the remains of classical antiquity. This was the decisive factor in Bramante's work in the last years of his life. We know from Vasari that he spent a great deal of time exploring the remains in Rome and in the surrounding countryside and it is safe to say that the gauntness and sheer size of many of these ruins impressed him deeply. In Milan he had already studied buildings like S. Lorenzo as well as some of the later churches in what is known as the Romano-Lombard style: in Rome he saw monuments such as the Basilica of Constantine and the Pantheon which were on a scale hitherto entirely outside his experience. Not only were such buildings impressively huge, they were also starkly simple. Most of the marble revetments of the great Baths and Basilicas had long since disappeared, exposing the concrete construction and the rough masonry which forced an architect to look at the constructional aspect rather than the decoration. The Pantheon had been converted into a Christian church – Sta Maria ad Martyres – as early as the seventh century, and this vast circular church, which retained much of its original decoration, is the ancestor of almost all sixteenth-century circular churches such as Bramante's own Tempietto. This was partly because of its size and grandeur, but mainly because the circular shape corresponded to the idea of the dedication – a *martyrium* was usually centrally planned (see p. 124).

[74]   Bramante's first work, the cloister at Sta Maria della Pace, is comparatively simple and has much in common with the cloister at S. Ambrogio in Milan. The Pace Cloister is on two floors of approximately equal height and is therefore partly conditioned by Roman buildings such as the Theatre of Marcellus. The most unusual feature is the way in which a column is made to stand immediately above the centres of each of the ground-floor arches. This has been much criticized, particularly by later sixteenth-century architects, since it breaks the rule of 'void over void, and solid over solid'. Nevertheless, it is evident that given the existing buildings which conditioned the heights of the two storeys, it would have been impossible to make single arches on the upper storey proportionate to those on the ground floor. What Bramante has done, therefore, is to adapt the scheme which he used in his Milanese cloister and to remove the wall on the upper floor leaving only the central member, which is transformed into a column instead of a pilaster. Some kind of support was essential at this point, since otherwise the entablature would be unable to support its own weight.

The effect of the Pace Cloister is gained entirely by subtle adjustments of proportion and by contrasts of light and shade, but his

74 Rome, Sta Maria della Pace, Cloister. Bramante, completed 1504

contemporary work at S. Pietro in Montorio is far more complicated   [75–77]
and of great importance for future developments. The Tempietto
was built for Ferdinand and Isabella of Spain on the spot which
traditionally saw the martyrdom of St Peter. As we learn from
Serlio's plate, Bramante's intention was to reorganize the whole   [77]
space of the courtyard in such a way that the tiny, centrally planned
church would have stood in the centre of a larger, centrally planned
cloister. This is very similar in spirit to such buildings as S. Satiro in
Milan, but the choice of a circular temple is of great importance. It
is often said that Italian sixteenth-century architects, in their passion
for centrally planned churches, were eagerly pursuing pagan ideals,
and it has even been maintained that Bramante's centrally planned
St Peter's represents a kind of triumph of worldliness. All this is based
on the false assumption that Christian churches must necessarily be

ROME, S. PIETRO
IN MONTORIO,
THE TEMPIETTO
by Bramante, 1502

75 Section and
elevation

76 Exterior

cruciform in plan. The earliest Christian churches were of two types, the *martyrium* and the *basilica*. Martyria were almost always small and almost always centrally planned. They were erected in places with some religious association, such as the spot where a martyrdom had taken place, or places in the Holy Land itself.[17] They did not serve as parish churches, but as commemorative monuments. The needs of a congregation were met by the basilica which, as we have seen, was the type of plan adopted by Brunelleschi and his followers,

following ancient precedent for parochial churches. It is clear, therefore, that to anyone interested in Early Christian antiquities and late antique architecture, there was only one possible solution for a commission to build a small church to mark the spot where St Peter was crucified. The Tempietto is therefore circular. The rest of it is conditioned by Bramante's desire to re-create antique forms in the service of modern Christian needs and the result, like Raphael's frescoes in the Vatican, is one of those High Renaissance works by which all others are judged. It is not without significance that, in 1570, Palladio, in his treatise on architecture, illustrated a great number of classical buildings and a considerable number of his own works, but the only other modern work was the Tempietto.

[75]

Even though the court as a whole was never completed it is still easy to see that the principal geometric effect depends on the combination of concentric circles in the plan with concentric cylinders in the elevation. The Tempietto itself consists of two cylinders – the peristyle and the cella – the peristyle being low and wide and the cella tall and narrow. The width of the peristyle is equal to the height of the cella, excluding the dome, and these simple proportional relationships can be traced throughout the building. The dome is hemispherical internally and externally[18] and is, therefore, proportioned to the height of the cella.

Several antique sources underlie the Tempietto, the most important being the small round temple near the Tiber (believed in the sixteenth century to be a temple of Vesta) and the famous Temple of the Sibyl at Tivoli, both of which have peristyles similar to that of the Tempietto – with an important exception. The temple at Tivoli is celebrated for the extreme richness of the frieze of its Corinthian order, whereas the Tempietto is the first modern building to employ the Tuscan order correctly. Vitruvius had pointed out that temples ought to be architecturally conformable to their dedications; in other words, that a temple dedicated to a virgin goddess ought to be of the Corinthian order, whereas Hercules or Mars demands the Doric. Alberti and, later, Palladio repeat this idea, so the notion was present to the minds of Renaissance architects, but Bramante was the first to put it into effect and to combine it with the martyrium theme. He used the Tuscan order – which is Roman Doric – because it was appropriate to the character of Peter, but he went further still in his treatment of the frieze.

126

There exists a fragment of the frieze from the Temple of Vespasian, carved with reliefs of various pagan sacrificial instruments and symbols. The Tempietto uses antique Tuscan columns of granite which Bramante supplied with new marble caps and bases. Because the Tuscan is a form of Doric the frieze is carved with alternating metopes and triglyphs. Closer examination reveals that the metopes are unlike those of the normal classical order, though like the frieze of the Temple of Vespasian in that they are carved with liturgical instruments – but these are the instruments of the Christian liturgy. There could hardly be a clearer exposition of Bramante's view that good modern architecture grew out of good ancient architecture in the same, organic, way as Christianity had grown out of the ancient world.

The Tempietto, therefore, in spite of its tiny size, contains the germ of Bramante's grandiose designs for the rebuilding of St Peter's; and it is a building which must be seen in this context if we are to understand Bramante's work and, through him, the whole of Italian sixteenth-century architecture.

ROME,
S. PIETRO IN MONTORIO,
THE TEMPIETTO
by Bramante, 1502

77 Plan showing proposed remodelling of the cloister

Raph Vrbinas ex Lapide Corcili Rome, exstructum
Annus ipsius ætat 1517

Another of his works occupies a comparable position in secular architecture, but unfortunately the building itself was destroyed in the seventeenth century and we have only a few drawings and engravings of it. Two of these, however, give a very good idea of the appearance of the palace, which is usually referred to as the House of Raphael. It is recorded by Vasari and was probably built by Bramante for himself, but was later lived in by Raphael. It stands in the same relationship to sixteenth-century palace design as the Tempietto does to later centrally planned churches and it is no exaggeration to say that for the next two centuries or more all Italian palaces can be related to it, even when they react against it. We have no precise date for it, but it was probably built late in Bramante's career, i.e. about 1512. Like the Tempietto, it is firmly based on a classical prototype, in this case the *insula*, or block of flats, built above a row of shops. These shops with flats above them were very numerous in ancient Rome and a few remains in Ostia have survived to this day to give us an idea of the type. As we have already seen in the evolution of Florentine palaces, the basic idea of a row of shops on the ground floor with living quarters above them was by no means new. What is new in the House of Raphael design is the simplification and strict symmetry.

[78, 79]

128

ROME, HOUSE OF
RAPHAEL
by Bramante, *c.* 1512

78 Elevation

79 Drawing by
Palladio (?)

It will be noticed at once that all the shops are identical on each side of the central axis. The ground floor has heavy rustication, and then a course of smooth stone separates it from the *piano nobile*, which is distinguished by the use of a Doric order and tabernacle frames to the windows. There is only one order and the upper storeys are done away with, giving the maximum contrast between the shops and the living quarters.[19] Every element is clearly distinguished from its neighbour: thus, the windows with their balconies do not touch the columns on either side and are not united with the string-course below them. All the windows have identical triangular pediments, so that once the basic element has been established it can be repeated. These principles – symmetry, repetition of identical elements, and clarity of function – are Bramante's main contribution to palace design.

Nevertheless, his most important works were carried out at the direct command of Julius II, and consist of the replanning and re-designing of new St Peter's as well as considerable work in the Vatican Palace. Unfortunately, most of his work in the Vatican has been altered almost beyond recognition, while St Peter's, as it exists today, has scarcely anything in common with what we can recon-struct of Bramante's original project. The present main courtyard in

129

the Vatican Palace, that of S. Damaso, was built by Bramante as a series of arcades not unlike those of the Colosseum, but the open spaces have been glazed in, to protect the frescoes by Raphael and his pupils in the loggia, and the original effect of light and shade is thus entirely lost.

A much grander undertaking was the enormous amphitheatre built for Julius II in deliberate imitation both of a classical amphitheatre and a classical villa. This is on three levels and stretches from the palace proper uphill towards a small summer-house known as the Belvedere. The entire scheme was about 300 yards in length and consisted of two long wings of buildings, three storeys high at the palace end and reducing to a single storey at the Belvedere end. The intermediate levels had elaborate ramps and staircases and the whole design ended in a curved wall leading into the Belvedere proper. The Belvedere was already in existence, and the great exedra disguises the fact that Bramante's end wall met the villa at an awkward angle. The whole vast scheme was never completed and was much altered in the sixteenth century. The subsequent building of a part of the Vatican Museum and Library across the courts has now made it impossible to see the scheme as it was originally intended to be seen, from the Stanze decorated by Raphael. The most important aspect of the Belvedere as it now exists lies in the treatment devised by Bramante for an immensely long expanse of plain walling. The texture of the side walls is enlivened by the contrast between the channelled joints of the masonry walling with the smooth surfaces of the arches and pilasters on top of it. The pilasters are paired, with a single break

[*80, 81*]

80 Rome, Vatican, Belvedere Court, by Bramante. Reconstruction by Ackerman

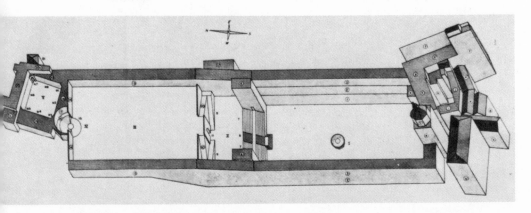

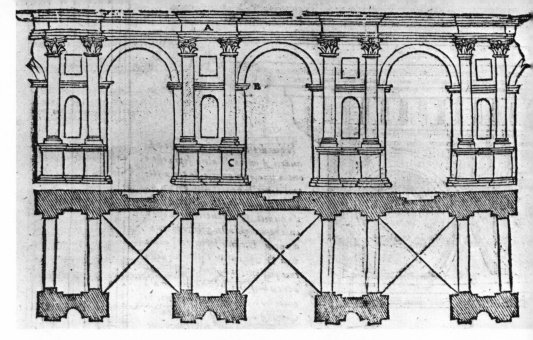

81 Rome, Vatican, Belvedere Court, by Bramante. Plan and elevation

forward of the entablature above them, although each pilaster retains
a separate base. Between each pair of pilasters is a round-headed arch,
the width of which is proportioned to the space between the pilasters
in such a way that the whole is divided according to the Golden
Section. The treatment is thus rather similar to Alberti's division of
the walls inside S. Andrea at Mantua, and both forms were very
widely copied by later architects.

All this, however, was put into the shade by the project to rebuild
St Peter's. Julius II was incomparably the greatest patron of the age,
capable of employing Bramante, Michelangelo, and Raphael simultaneously and on work which brought out their highest powers.
Bramante's St Peter's, had it ever been executed, would have been
a worthy companion for Michelangelo's Sistine Chapel or Raphael's
Stanze and would have surpassed both in sheer grandeur of conception.

By the middle of the fifteenth century it was already becoming
evident that Old St Peter's, which was then more than a thousand
years old, was in a very bad state. Nicholas V began some foundations
for a rebuilding of the choir, but after his death in 1455 nothing
more was done until the election of Julius II in 1503. Even then it

seems that Julius's original intention was little more than to continue to prop up the old basilica and to rebuild only where absolutely necessary. The old basilica was hallowed by its association with the first Christian Emperor as well as the tomb of St Peter and no Pope less self-confident than Julius II could have brought himself to destroy it entirely in favour of a new building. Nevertheless, by about the summer of 1505 Julius and Bramante between them must have decided that they had the opportunity to rebuild the greatest church in Western Christendom – Hagia Sophia having fallen to the Turks in 1453 – on a truly heroic, Roman scale, and to re-create the whole as a vast domed space. This much, at least, we can infer from the medal struck to commemorate the laying of the foundation-stone

[82, 83] on 18 April 1506 and from the drawing which is thought to be Bramante's original project and which is, unfortunately, the only surviving drawing that can be regarded as certainly by him. The importance of the inscription on the foundation medal – TEMPLI PETRI INSTAVRACIO – can hardly be over-estimated, since *instaurare* means 'to restore, to revive, to bring to completion' and is often used in this sense in Church Latin. This makes it clear that the intention was to restore the Constantinian basilica to itself rather than to sweep it away and replace it with something new.

Unfortunately, the building history of St Peter's is exceedingly complicated and we have no documents for the earliest years. We do not even know exactly when Bramante was first commissioned to make new designs: indeed, the most difficult problem arises from the fact that he seems never to have been given specific instructions, in the sense in which a modern architect is given a brief to design a building of such-and-such dimensions at such-and-such a cost. It is

ROME, ST PETER'S
by Bramante

82 Foundation medal by
Caradosso, 1506

83 Bramante's plan
(Uffizi no. 1)

essential to realize that, for Bramante as well as for Julius, what really mattered was the symbolism of the building, the enclosure of the Tomb of the Prince of the Apostles in a basilica of a type which would have been acknowledged as classical by the original fourth-century architects. The problem is greatly complicated by the fact that Bramante's drawing might well be for a rebuilding of the choir only, an extension to the existing church not unlike that which he had added to Sta Maria delle Grazie in Milan. Nevertheless, it is usually assumed that his original ideas were for a centrally planned building and that the Latin cross projects which finally triumphed were imposed upon him by the clergy. It is true that a Latin cross building has many liturgical advantages, particularly because it provides a greater space for processions, and these practical advantages were almost certainly the reason for the eventual modification of the present basilica into a Latin cross type. It is, however, quite wrong to suppose that the Latin cross type represents a 'religious' type of plan while the central plan is 'secular' or even 'pagan'. The idea that the rebuilding of this unique monument could be a subject of purely architectural interest and that Bramante and Julius II were trying to re-create it in a pagan form betrays a complete misunderstanding of the development of Italian architecture, of Bramante's art and, above all, of Julius II.

Bramante's project is directly derived from the Tempietto in that he was designing, on an enormous scale, a martyrium. Further, he wished to associate an Early Christian basilica with this martyrium, thus redesigning an ancient Roman building within the same framework as that which had limited Constantine's architects in the fourth century. Constantine's other foundations, the Holy Sepulchre and

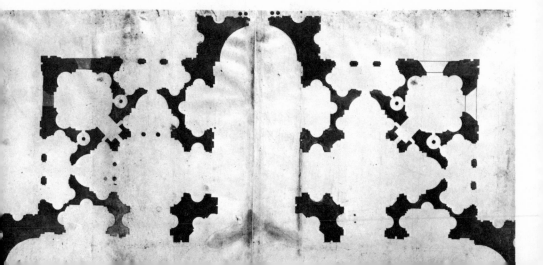

the Church of the Nativity, also combined a martyrium with a basilica. In addition to this we know that, for Bramante's generation, the mathematical perfection of a central plan had a theological symbolism in that it reflected the perfection of God. For that generation the cruciform symbolism of a Latin cross church was rather obvious; but we know that more than half a century later, at the time of the Council of Trent, the medieval cruciform type of church came once more to be preferred, and this change of taste probably had some effect on the changes in the design for St Peter's itself.

When Bramante died he left no definitive design to bind his designated successor, Raphael. Little had been built beyond the foundations of the main piers and the setting-out of the great arches linking the piers. These two factors, however, condition the scale of the present building, so that all his successors as Capomaestro were bound by his sense of the heroic; but it must be admitted that his lack of experience of work on this colossal scale led him into designing piers which were totally inadequate to support the weights he would have placed on them. Since no mason had any practical experience of this type of work there was no one to guide him, and all his successors found themselves constantly forced to enlarge the piers and to provide more and more abutment for the thrust of the dome, which, had it been built to Bramante's original design would have required even more support than the present building provides. In spite of the fact that there was no definitive design it is possible to gain a fairly precise idea of Bramante's intentions at the end of his life and to contrast them with those at the beginning of the work.

Apart from the autograph drawing in the Uffizi and the foundation medal there are numerous drawings which can be associated with Bramante's office – many in the hand of his assistant and successor, Baldassare Peruzzi – and there have recently come to light some interesting drawings attributed to Menicantonio de' Chiarellis, who was for many years associated with the Fabbrica di S. Pietro. [84] His sketchbook (now in the Morgan Library, New York) contains at least one drawing which seems to confirm the statement, made in the sixteenth century, that Bramante made a wooden model. If such a model existed, it seems perverse to maintain that Bramante left no definitive design. This is not so, since it is easy to demonstrate the confusion over Bramante's intentions which existed in the minds of his contemporaries and collaborators.

134

To begin with, the drawing in the Uffizi is usually reproduced as a central plan, in the form shown in plate 89. Evidence for this interpretation can be found in the foundation medal and the Menicantonio drawing, as well as in the existence of numerous variations on this centrally planned theme, by architects such as Giuliano da Sangallo, who was certainly connected with the Fabbrica in some way rather hard to define with precision. Similarly, there is evidence for the view that Bramante intended only to add a tribune to the existing nave, rather like his tribune at Sta Maria delle Grazie, and [70] that he then intended to replace the original nave with a new one, retaining, therefore, the Latin cross plan. Evidence for this, apart from the existence of Sta Maria delle Grazie, can also be found in the fact that the Uffizi drawing is only a half-plan, and, especially, in the fact [83] that Raphael – according to Serlio – made a Latin cross design. Serlio's evidence is particularly important. He was about thirty at the time when Bramante was making his first designs for St Peter's, so he was a contemporary, and, more important, he had a long

84 Rome, St Peter's. Drawing by Menicantonio de' Chiarellis (?)

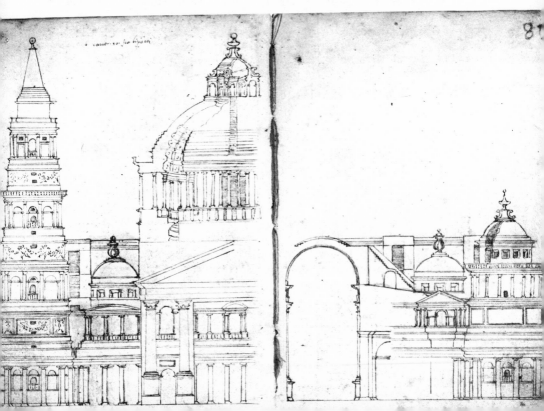

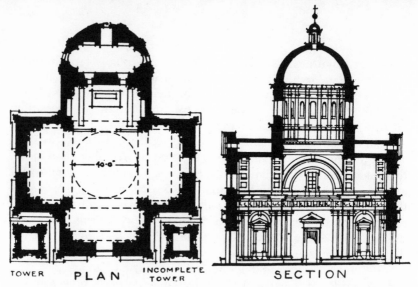

TOWER   **PLAN**   INCOMPLETE TOWER   **SECTION**

85 Montepulciano, S. Biagio, by Antonio da Sangallo the Elder, 1518–45. Plan and section

association with Peruzzi, whose drawings he inherited. Yet Serlio reproduces in his treatise a central plan, which he associates with Peruzzi, and a Latin cross plan, which he associates with Raphael.

There is, however, another category of evidence altogether. This consists of the churches which can be regarded as derived from one or other of Bramante's projects. Some are known to have been designed by him, or under his direct supervision, while others were produced by men not known to have been connected with him, but clearly under the influence of his architectural ideas. The principal [94] examples are the churches of S. Biagio alla Pagnotta, SS. Celso e Giuliano, and S. Eligio degli Orefici, all in Rome, and the Madonna [85–87] di S. Biagio at Montepulciano, and Sta Maria della Consolazione at Todi.

S. Biagio and SS. Celso e Giuliano were designed by Bramante himself, as trials for St Peter's, but unfortunately neither church now exists in its original form. SS. Celso e Giuliano was very similar to plate 89, i.e. to the centrally planned version of the Uffizi drawing, but it seems also to have had an emphasis on one side that would have turned it into a 'directed central plan', or one which has a definite orientation. S. Biagio alla Pagnotta was similar, but with a true nave, two bays in length, attached to the central domical space. This idea of a great dome with a nave tacked on to it, which goes back at least

136

to the Cathedral of Florence, is also found in drawings by Fra Giocondo and Giuliano da Sangallo, both of whom had charge of the building of St Peter's at the time of Bramante's last illness and death (1513–14).

S. Eligio degli Orefici was probably designed by Raphael and Bramante together, and has much in common with the grandiose basilica in Raphael's *School of Athens*, which dates from this time. S. Eligio was finished by Peruzzi, and it is difficult to say exactly where it stands in the development of St Peter's (see page 143); but there can be no doubt that the splendid church of the Madonna di S. Biagio at Montepulciano, in Tuscany, is directly influenced by Bramante's ideas for St Peter's. It was built by Antonio da Sangallo the Elder, the younger brother of Giuliano and the uncle of Antonio the Younger, between 1518 and 1545, by reason, as Vasari says, of the miracles wrought there, which explains why it is a martyrium in shape. The plan is very like that of Giuliano's Sta Maria delle Carceri at Prato, except for the significant fact that it has the east end

[94]

[85–87]

86, 87 Montepulciano, S. Biagio, by Antonio da Sangallo the Elder

Questo è il diritto di dentro, & di fuori della pianta passata, dal qual si può comprendere la gran massa, & il gran peso che saria questo edificio sopra a quattro massa (sì come io dissi anti) doueria mettere pensiero ad ogni prudente Architetto a farla al piano di terra, non che in tanta altezza: & però io giudico, che l'Architetto dee esser più presto alquanto timido che troppo animoso: perche se sarà timido, egli farà le sue cose ben sicure, & anco non sdegnerà di uolere il consiglio d'altri, e così facendo rare volte perirà: ma se sarà troppo animoso, egli non uorrà l'altrui consiglio: anzi si considerà solamente nel suo ingegno, onde spesse volte precipitaranno le cose da lui fatte. & però io concludo che la troppo animosità proceda dalla presuntione, & la presuntione dal poco sapere: ma che la timidità sia cosa uirtuosa, dandosi sempre a credere di sapere o nulla, o poco. Le misure di questa opera si trouerranno con i palmi piccioli, che sono qui a dietro.

ROME, ST PETER'S

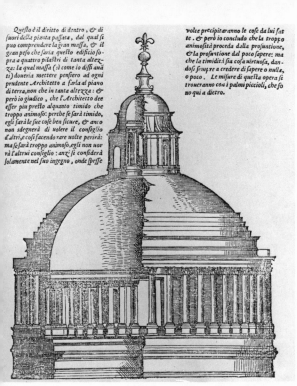

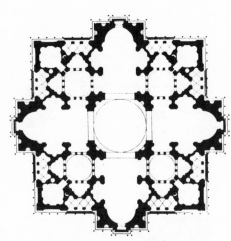

88 Bramante's dome, section and elevation   89 Bramante's first plan

90 Model by Antonio da Sangallo the Younger

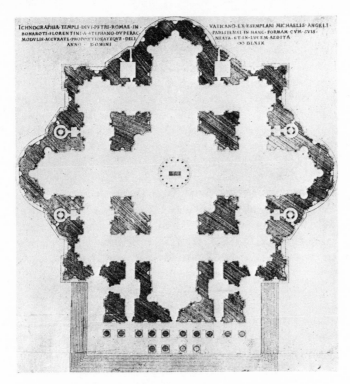

91 Michelangelo's plan

extended into an apsidal form and the west end marked by two grand campanili (only one of which was completed). Thus, it is very similar in disposition to one possible interpretation of Bramante's St Peter's [82] as shown on the foundation medal. Internally, it has a simple, austere, majesty which sets it in a different class from Sta Maria delle Carceri, and indeed from any other known work of the Sangallo family. The suspicion that it must reflect Bramante's own ideas grows to near-certainty when we compare it with the Madonna della Consolazione at Todi, in Umbria, ostensibly by the almost unknown architect Cola da Caprarola. In fact, it is known that Peruzzi had a share in the building, after Bramante's death, and the plan is an almost exact repetition of a drawing made in Milan, many years [64] earlier, by Leonardo. From all these pieces of evidence it is therefore possible to reconstruct one or two of the stages of Bramante's thought concerning St Peter's.

139

After his death in 1514 Bramante was succeeded as Capomaestro by Raphael and Peruzzi, both of whom produced the variant plans known to us from Serlio, but neither of whom seems to have done much actual construction. The Sack of Rome by the Imperial troops in 1527 effectively stopped all building for many years, and in the 1530s the drawings made by the Dutch artist Maerten van Heemskerck show that the great shell impressed him in the same way as the other ruins of Rome. It was during this period that Antonio da Sangallo the Younger – who had also worked under Bramante – began to redesign the building as a whole and to repair the damages caused by long neglect. The central space was fixed by the fact that Bramante's piers already existed, but Sangallo very much enlarged them and at the same time designed a new shape of dome, rather like a beehive, which would have been much easier to construct. There is an

[90]   engraving and a large wooden model of this project made in the last years of Sangallo's life. Fortunately, his death in 1546 prevented the execution, since Sangallo's model shows very clearly that all of Bramante's immediate successors were unable to think on the heroic scale and relied rather weakly on a series of compromise solutions. Thus, the model shows an awkward compromise between the central plan and the longitudinal form which was Raphael's contribution to the design just before 1520. The desire to combine the virtues of the central plan with the practical advantages of the Latin cross can be traced back to Bramante's own lifetime, and it was still to exert great influence on Michelangelo, who succeeded Sangallo on 1 January 1547, more than thirty years after the death of Bramante. In spite of the fact that they had never been friendly, Michelangelo expressed his intention of returning to a basically Bramantesque form, which he did in a very elaborate and very subtle reduction of Bramante's plan to a combination of central plan and Latin cross expressed in

[91]   Mannerist terms. Principally, this means that where Bramante had conceived his central plan as a square shape with the entrance in any of the four straight sides, Michelangelo stood the square on one corner and obtained a diamond shape, using the corner as the main facade and emphasizing it by blunting the point and adding a very large portico. Comparison of the two plans shows, further, that Michelangelo reduced the overall size, increased the size of the main piers, and reduced the open spaces between the piers and the outside walls. By this drastic reduction and compression he ensured the

140

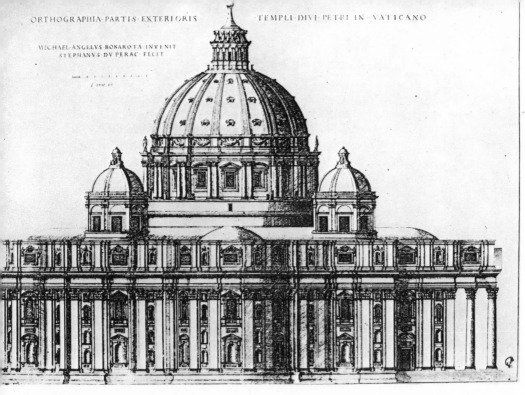

92 Rome, St Peter's, Michelangelo's design for the exterior

stability of the building and provided adequate support for the dome, even though he abandoned the idea of building Bramante's dome and constantly modified his own projects and models. [88]

He pressed ahead with the construction with more vigour than had been shown for nearly forty years, so that when he died, in 1564, a considerable part of the basilica was standing in the form in which we know it, and the drum had been completed as far as the springing of the dome. The dome itself is one of the problems of St Peter's. It is known that Michelangelo, at one stage, wished it to be a hemisphere, like Bramante's design, but with heavily accented ribs corre- [92] sponding to the main lines of his wall-treatment. This would have been a more dynamic treatment than Bramante's smooth shell, expressive of the difference in temperament of the two men, as well as of the great change that came over architectural ideals in the half-century between Bramante's death and Michelangelo's.

141

Michelangelo, however, also projected a dome in a slightly pointed
[1]   form, and this was the shape adopted by the builders. As with
Brunelleschi's dome, the pointed shape exerts less thrust, and it was
this which was decisive when, between 1585 and 1590, it was built
by Giacomo della Porta with the assistance of Domenico Fontana,
who was probably the best engineer of the day. Michelangelo's own
conception of the building, unlike Bramante's, was dynamic; and
from the back of the church it is still possible to gain some idea of
the effect he sought. Here the giant pilasters are linked together,
[92]   rather like those in Bramante's Belvedere, to form single vertical
units which link up with the ribs of the dome and give an almost
Gothic effect of verticality. The ribs of the present dome are fundamentally those projected by Michelangelo, but are probably slightly
thinner and more graceful in their general effect.

Once again, however, the plan was profoundly modified and the
[93]   present Latin cross shape of the building is the result of a transformation wrought in the first half of the seventeenth century by Carlo
Maderna. He not only decorated much of the interior, but he also
extended and changed Michelangelo's plan by the addition of a long
nave and then a façade made necessary by the extension. Finally, the
new design was made into one of the masterpieces of Baroque by the
completion of the layout of the great piazza and the superbly
theatrical effect of the Tuscan colonnade with scores of statues on a
gigantic scale, designed by Bernini and built from 1656 onwards.

93 Rome, St Peter's. Plan as built

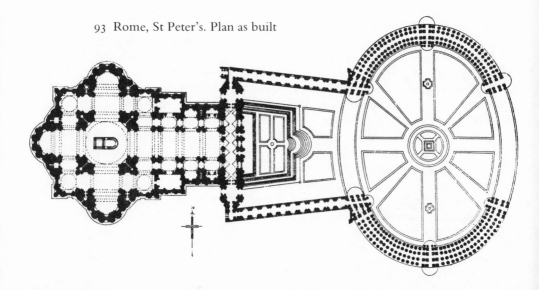

CHAPTER SEVEN

Raphael and Giulio Romano

Raphael may have been related to Bramante. It would seem reasonable that Bramante himself, as soon as he realized the magnitude of the task he had undertaken at St Peter's, began to look around for a capable successor; and, although most of the major architects of the next generation worked under him at one time or another, his choice fell upon Raphael. It seems likely that the two were working closely together by 1509, for Raphael's fresco of the *School of Athens* is set in a building so like Bramante's original projects for St Peter's that it is usually thought to reflect his direct inspiration. In the same year the little Roman church of S. Eligio degli Orefici (which is a tiny [94] Greek cross and therefore a possible experiment for St Peter's) was designed by Bramante and Raphael and carried out from 1514 onwards, the dome probably being finished by Peruzzi. Raphael died at the age of thirty-seven, in 1520, so that his surveyorship of the works at St Peter's was neither as long nor as important as might reasonably have been expected. Nevertheless, in the six last hectic years of his life, apart from his enormous output as a painter, Raphael seems to have found time to design three palaces, a chapel, and a villa and to have determined, to some extent, a new trend in architecture somewhat similar to the development in his very last pictures. To put the matter in another way, both as a painter and as an architect Raphael seems to move in his last years away from the serene classicism of his own *School of Athens*, which is the equivalent of Bramante's mature style, towards a richer and at the same time more dramatic style which is the beginning of Mannerism. This can be seen in the chapel he built in Sta Maria del Popolo for the wealthy Sienese banker, Agostino Chigi, where there is far greater richness than in S. Eligio, although the structural forms are almost identical. Perhaps more important still were the two palaces he built in Rome, both of which diverge from the prototype which was his own house. The Palazzo Vidoni-Caffarelli still exists in the centre of Rome, but [95] has been much enlarged.[20] Nevertheless, the basic elements, the rusticated basement, the *piano nobile* with columns and an attic storey

143

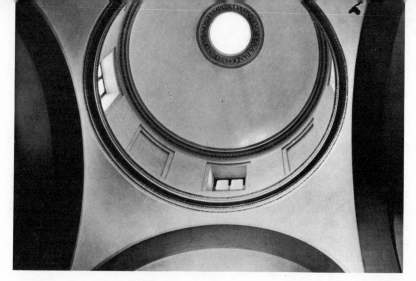

94 Rome, S. Eligio degli Orefici. Dome

above, do not vary very significantly from the House of Raphael type; but his next palace, which may date from the last year of his life, is [96] altogether different. This was the Palazzo Branconio dell'Aquila and is known to us only from drawings and an engraving. Here the differences are essential, and an analysis will make clear the principles of the new style, known as Mannerism.

The façade of the Palazzo Branconio dell'Aquila should be com- [78] pared with that of the House of Raphael in order to see the differences which, though apparently quite small, affect the architect's whole outlook. To begin with, it is clear that the Palazzo Branconio is very much richer in texture, and particularly in the amount of decoration which has been applied to the surface. In the House of Raphael the decoration is virtually confined to such things as balustrades and pediments over the windows, which are in themselves structural features; or it is a matter of contrast in texture between the rustication of the ground floor and the smooth wall of the *piano nobile*. Even here, it is possible to argue that this textural contrast gives a feeling of greater solidity to the lower part of the building and is to that extent structural also. The decoration on the façade of the Palazzo Branconio cannot be said to be structural at all, and it is this which is the essential element of distinction. Perhaps the most important example is the way in which the columns have been moved from the *piano nobile* down to the ground floor, in itself reasonable enough,

144

since the columns can then be said to be supporting the upper part of the building. This is precisely what they do not do, since each of the columns has an empty niche immediately above it, and we get an uncomfortable feeling of a massive support with a void above it. It is true that in at least one of the drawings which record the appearance of the palace these niches are filled with statues; nevertheless, such massive Doric columns ought to appear to have more to do than simply to support small statues. In the same way, it is evident that the pattern of the windows on the *piano nobile*, with their alternation of triangular and segmental pediments, form a part of the wall surface and are tied together by an entablature which has no order to support it except the columns of the tabernacle windows themselves. The arrangement of the *piano nobile* contrasts most strikingly with the repetition of the identical units in the House of Raphael, since it has a highly complex rhythm of niches, triangular and segmental pedimented windows, as well as the decorative swags. This extreme richness coupled with a deliberate inversion of the functions of the architectural elements – columns supporting nothing – are characteristic of the stylistic trend which began in Raphael's lifetime and which was to dominate all the arts in Italy for the rest of the century.

Mannerism, as a term, was invented some sixty years ago when it became clear that the purely classical style of Bramante and of Raphael and Peruzzi at the beginning of their careers was not the same in intention as the style practised by Giulio Romano or even by Raphael and Peruzzi in their last years. Similar tendencies can be found in painting and in sculpture, perhaps most notably in Raphael's

95 Rome, Palazzo Vidoni-Caffarelli. Elevation

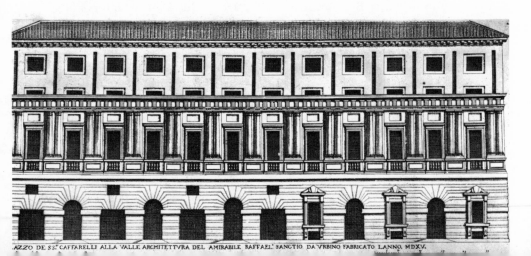

AZZO DE SS.ͬ CAFFARELLI ALLA VALLE ARCHITETTVRA DEL AMIRABILE RAFFAEL SANCTIO DA VRBINO FABRICATO L.ANNO, MDXV.

late work such as the *Transfiguration* (in the Vatican). In all three arts this new, restless, style was due to a number of factors of which the most important were the personality of Michelangelo and the fact that the classic style of Bramante and of the early Raphael must have seemed to younger men a dead end. It must have appeared to them that nothing could be done on those lines which would be better than work already in existence, so that rather than try to rival Bramante's Tempietto or Raphael's *School of Athens* the sensible thing to do seemed to be to try to find a different, more exciting, style. In architecture the mere imitation of classical prototypes was now quite simple and it seemed worth experimenting with the classical vocabulary in order to find new combinations which might yield results visually as satisfactory as anything which had come down from antiquity. Many other factors contributed to the rise and spread of Mannerist art: the Marxist explanation of the movement in terms of the political and economic crises which culminated in the Sack of Rome in 1527 and the growing crisis of the Reformation and Counter-Reformation which divided Europe throughout the whole of the sixteenth and seventeenth centuries, is undoubtedly valid for some part of the phenomenon. It is, however, totally inadequate as an explanation of the whole because Raphael's *Transfiguration* was left unfinished at his death, long before the Sack of Rome, and also because perhaps the finest of all Mannerist buildings is the Palazzo del Tè at Mantua. This was built by Giulio Romano from 1524 onwards, in a town which was scarcely affected by the political upheaval.

Mannerism as a term is useful as a means of distinguishing a phase between the conscious classical harmony aimed at by an artist like Bramante and the passionate drama of the Baroque style which is epitomized by Bernini. Most of the art produced in the intervening century is in one way or another sophisticated, frustrated, and sometimes even downright neurotic. For this reason the term 'Mannerism' must be retained, although it is necessary to bear in mind that many artists, such as Giulio Romano, thought of themselves as practising a classical style and many of the features in Giulio's work can indeed be traced back to Roman architecture of the Imperial period. What is interesting about this is the way in which the changed intentions of the sixteenth-century architects led them to look for features in antique architecture which had been neglected by their predecessors;

FACCIATA DEL PALAZZO ET HABBITATIONE DI RAFAELE SANTIO DA VRBINO SV LA VIA DI BORGHONOVO FABRICATO
CON SVO DISEGNIO L'ANNO MD·XIII·IIII Scala Palmi Quaranta
CIRCA·ESEGVITO DA BRAMANTE DA VRBINO

96 Rome, Palazzo
Branconio dell'Aquila.
Engraving after
destroyed building by
Raphael

97 Rome, Palazzo
Spada. A mid
16th-century palace
based on Raphael's
Palazzo Branconio

98 Florence, Palazzo Pandolfini

and it is quite wrong to imagine that, because they appreciated things in Imperial Roman art which had not appealed to Bramante or to Raphael, they were therefore insensitive to classical precedents. Indeed, almost the opposite might be maintained, for the first great treatises on architecture, those by Serlio, Palladio, and Vignola, were all written at this time and all take it for granted that classical antiquity is the foundation of architectural style. They are thus in the direct line of descent from Alberti's treatise, but all three were writing books which were intended to be textbooks for architects, rather than a treatise on aesthetics, as Alberti's tends to be.

[98]   Raphael also designed the Palazzo Pandolfini in Florence. This is a simpler version of the Palazzo Branconio adapted to Florentine taste and adapted also to the idea of a villa standing in the country rather than a palace in a town, since it was built on the outskirts of Florence, near the Porta S. Gallo. The development of the villa is of particular importance in Italian sixteenth-century architecture since on the one hand it looks back to the villas of the Romans, as described by Pliny, and, on the other, it looks forward to a whole class (including the English country-house) which derives directly from the

principles to be laid down by Palladio. One of the first and certainly one of the finest of these villas was begun about 1516 by Raphael and others, who included Antonio da Sangallo the Elder and Giulio Romano. This, which was never more than half finished, is the Villa Madama on the slopes of Monte Mario just outside Rome. There [99–101] seems no doubt that the original intention was to re-create a classical villa with an enormous circular courtyard in the centre and with a great garden like an amphitheatre terraced into the hillside. In fact, only half the building was ever erected so that the deep curve of the present entrance façade was intended to be half of the central circular court. Nevertheless, the Villa Madama, with its classical intentions, is a work of primary importance since the loggia at the back, now glazed in, contains the most magnificent surviving decoration carried out by Raphael and his pupils in direct imitation of the Golden House of Nero. The great loggia consists of three bays, those at either end being covered with quadripartite vaulting and the one in the centre with a domical vault. At one end (the one shown in plate 100) the wall is recessed into the hillside in a deep apse-like shape with a richly decorated half-dome over it. The whole of the decoration is carried out in low relief with strong, bright colour contrasting with dazzling white plaster, and it is easy to see how this must have seemed to contemporaries not only to resemble the fabulous Golden House of Nero but also in some senses to surpass it. From this it was a logical step for a young artist such as Giulio Romano, who carried out much of the decoration in the Villa Madama, to think that there was no point in merely continuing such a style, and that it was better to seek for new inventions of his own. This he did at the Palazzo del Tè.

Giulio Romano, as his name implies, was Roman born and was the first major artist to be born in the city for centuries. He was Raphael's pupil and his artistic executor and must have been exceedingly precocious, since it seems that he was born as late as 1499.[21] At any rate, Giulio Romano was Raphael's principal assistant some years before 1520 and a considerable share of the actual execution of the later frescoes in the Vatican and of the later paintings such as the *Transfiguration* or the *Holy Family under the Oak Tree* is very generally attributed to Giulio rather than to Raphael. Yet it must be said that Raphael, however pressed by his numerous commissions, would not have allowed Giulio to alter the basic style of the Raphael workshop

149

unless he himself was changing his own style in a similar way. Immediately after Raphael's death in 1520 Giulio Romano was commissioned to complete the Vatican frescoes and presumably also to supervise the completion of outstanding oil-paintings, among them the *Transfiguration*. He remained in Rome until 1524 and during these four years he worked as an architect, since there are two palaces in Rome which are reasonably attributed to him – the Palazzo Cicciaporci and the Palazzo Maccarani.

In 1524 Giulio went to Mantua to work for the Duke, Federigo Gonzaga, in whose service he remained until his death in 1546. His masterpiece is undoubtedly the Palazzo del Tè which was under construction by November 1526 and was completed about 1534. [*102–7*] This, like the Villa Madama, was a re-creation of a classical *villa suburbana*.[22] The palace in the city of Mantua is a gigantic building, but Federigo Gonzaga had a famous stable and he decided to build himself a villa just outside the town, which would be the headquarters of his stud and at the same time a place with a beautiful garden in which to pass a day in the heat of the summer. There are no bedrooms since the villa is only a mile or so from the Gonzaga palace. The plan shows the typical layout of a Roman villa; that is, four long, low, ranges enclosing a central square court. This is confirmed at first glance by the appearance of the entrance façade; but it is at this [*103*] point that one realizes that the Palazzo del Tè is by no means a simple building, and that what appears to be a straightforward classical villa is a most sophisticated structure. To take the plan first, it will be seen [*102*] that the principle of symmetrical disposition is not observed, for the building has four different ranges and the axis of the garden and the main garden front leads to a side door while the axis of the main entrance is at right angles to the garden. It might be argued that this was due to the exigencies of the site, but a closer examination shows that the building as a whole is full of surprises and contradictions

ROME, VILLA MADAMA
by Raphael, Antonio da Sangallo the Elder,
Giulio Romano and others, begun *c.* 1516

 99 Façade
100 Loggia
101 Plan

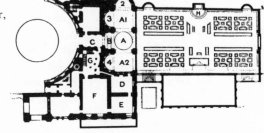

which are obviously intentional and were intended to appeal to a highly sophisticated taste, since most of the established rules of architecture are deliberately flouted in such a way that the educated spectator is intended to feel a thrill of delighted horror. This can be seen at once in the main entrance front which should be compared with the west side entrance, both of which should then be compared with the garden front. In each case, elements of one front are repeated but transformed in both others.

[104]

The main entrance front is a long, low, block with three equal arches in the centre and with four window bays apparently symmetrically disposed on either side. The wall is rusticated and articulated by Tuscan pilasters carrying a richly carved entablature. About three-quarters of the way up the pilasters there is a string-course which serves as sills for the attic windows. Almost the first thing one notices about this articulation is that the string-course is level with the face of the pilasters, forms the sill of the attic windows, and is tied into the keystone of the windows on the main floor. In other words, where Bramante took trouble to keep each element separate and distinct, here they seem to be deliberately combined in a surface pattern. The next glance, however, will reveal greater oddities than this, for the spacing of the pilasters is by no means equal. To the right of the entrance arches there is a wide bay, but the corresponding bay to the left is not only narrower, it also has the window off-centre. This might be thought to be no more than an oversight on the part of the designer, though it would be a strange oversight in so important a building by so highly trained an architect. Next, we notice that the three entrance bays are flanked on each side by three window bays and then there comes a caesura in the form of a pair of pilasters with a small niche set in a smooth wall between them. After this there follows a normal window bay and, finally, the façade is closed by a pair of pilasters. Thus, reading from the central arch of the entrance the rhythm is A A B B B C B, the last being differentiated from the other bays by the fact that it has paired pilasters at either side. The design is therefore both very subtle and consciously asymmetrical, but the full sophistication of this architecture can be realized only by moving round to the side front where a similar but not quite identical articulation is adopted, with the small niche bays framing the sides of the single entrance arch. More subtle still is the fact that the spectator is supposed to keep in mind the basic dis-

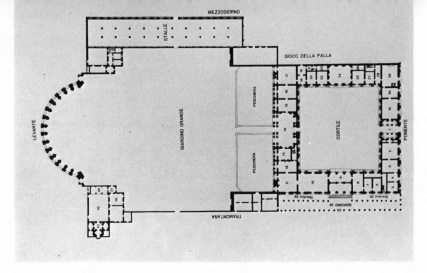

102 Mantua, Palazzo del Tè. Giulio Romano, *c.* 1526–34. Plan

position of the external fronts when he arrives on the garden side
which has, once more, a disposition around three large arches in the   [*106*]
centre. Here, however, the texture of the wall is quite different since
it is rusticated only up to the level of the bridge which runs across
the moat, now unfortunately dry. The main storey has smooth
walling and no attic, but has instead a totally different textural effect
obtained by a series of round arches carried on piers and columns in
a complicated rhythm. The larger arches of the centre are further
emphasized by a triangular pediment above them. Comparing the
entrance and garden fronts we see that they have in common a
triplet of arches in the centre, followed by three window bays on
each side, which are then followed by an odd small bay with a niche
separating the main windows from the final bay, which repeats the
form of the original three. Thus, what at first sight are two totally
different fronts, have the same underlying motives and there can be
no doubt that the architect intended this to create in the spectator's
mind a pleasure similar to that given by variations on a theme in
music. If, in imagination, we fill the moat with water so that in the
Italian sun the whole play of reflected light is cast up from the surface
of the water into the shallow arches above the garden windows, we
shall see how extremely subtle the architectural invention of Giulio
Romano was. The same can be said of some further points in the
building; for example, the precise articulation of these arches on the

153

103 Main façade

105 Part of inner
elevation of court

106 Garden front

104 Side door

MANTUA,
PALAZZO DEL TÈ
by Giulio Romano,
c. 1526–34

107 Atrium, looking
into the garden

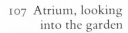

garden side. The four great columns which support the main arches of the garden front give the effect of massy supports carrying a considerable weight so that the arches and the vaulting of this portico, which in itself is markedly reminiscent of the Villa Madama, seem to be adequate for their task and disposed with symmetrical harmony. There are columns in the centre groups and columns and piers at the ends. The smaller window bays, however, are rather more complex in their disposition since we begin with what is generally, but erroneously, known as a Palladian[23] motive; that is, a semicircular arch supported on columns with a rectangular opening at either side formed by the entablature and another column. The window bay nearest the main entrance is such a motive and so is the second. At this point, however, the third window becomes a round-headed arch supported not on columns but on square piers, and the side spaces are omitted. This motive is followed by the small niche bay, and then the last of the arches repeats this new type of window. By comparison with the main entrance front, therefore, there is a further complication in the disposition of the bays which, reading from the centre arch, are now A A B B C D C. In fact, the whole of the Palazzo del Tè is full of this sort of sophistication, which explains why it became immensely famous as soon as it was built and has always been regarded as Giulio Romano's masterpiece.

[107]

Two other things about it need to be recorded. Firstly, the sides of the internal court do not correspond precisely with any of the exterior sides but have rhythms and complications of their own. What is even odder is the treatment of some details which, to our eyes, are not particularly startling, but must have seemed strange to contemporaries and are essential elements in the conception of Mannerism. Some of the keystones in the window arches appear to slip down into the space of the arch itself, thus contradicting the impression of stability which the keystone of an arch is normally intended to give. This feeling of insecurity can be seen still more clearly in the entablature of the internal court, where Giulio has actually allowed a number of the triglyphs to appear to have slipped down into the wall space below, creating a definite feeling of unease in the mind of the spectator. This deliberate malaise is generally regarded as the hall-mark of Mannerist art on account of its contrast with the serenity of Bramante's architecture or the passion and confidence of the Baroque.

[105]

[105]

156

The second important feature of the Palazzo del Tè confirms this impression. The interior decoration was largely executed by Giulio Romano and a number of his pupils, and some of it is of the utmost delicacy of execution, comparable with its prototype the Villa Madama. The most important of the decorative features, however, the so-called Room of the Giants, is totally different in character and rather crude in execution. This extraordinary room, mostly painted between March 1532 and July 1534, has been fully described by Vasari, who was shown over it by Giulio himself. Briefly, it consists of a small room, with almost no light, in which the angles of the floor and the walls and the ceiling have all been softened and then painted so that the first impression is that one does not know where the walls end and the ceiling begins. The paintings are remarkable in themselves. The whole of the ceiling is covered by a representation of a great circular temple floating, apparently suspended in space, above the spectator's head with the Assembly of the Gods and with Jupiter hurling a thunderbolt towards the earth. This, the region in which we find ourselves, is a scene of utter chaos, for the rebellion of the Giants against Olympus is taking place all round us and the Giants are being crushed by huge blocks of stone, buildings, and rocks which have been hurled down on them by the Gods in the ceiling. This rather unpleasant scene is much heightened by the devices of illusionism and perspective which Giulio had mastered under Raphael; in this particular case, he was competing with the most famous of all his predecessors in this field, Mantegna. Mantegna's great feat of illusionism was the Camera degli Sposi in the Palazzo Ducale of Mantua itself. The great difference between the two lies in the intentions of the artist, since Mantegna's illusionism is charming, care-free, and plausible where Giulio's has as its sole end the striking of terror into the spectator and the exhibition of the artist's virtuosity. A quotation from Vasari will illustrate this point, bearing in mind that Vasari was here repeating Giulio's own explanations:

Besides this, through an opening in the darkness of a grotto, which reveals a distant landscape painted with beautiful judgment, may be seen many Giants flying, all smitten by the thunderbolts of Jove, and, as it were, on the point of being overwhelmed at that moment by the fragments of the mountains, like the others. In another part Giulio depicted other Giants, upon whom temples, columns, and other pieces of buildings are collapsing, making a vast slaughter and havoc of those proud beings. And in this part, among those falling fragments of buildings, stands the fireplace of the room, which, when there is a fire in it, makes it appear as if the Giants are burning, for Pluto is painted there, flying towards the centre with his chariot drawn by lean horses, and accompanied by the Furies of Hell; and thus Giulio, not departing from the subject of the story with this invention of the fire, made a most beautiful adornment for the fireplace.

In this work, moreover, in order to render it the more fearsome and terrible, Giulio represented the Giants, huge and fantastic in aspect, falling to the earth, smitten in various ways by the lightnings and thunderbolts; some in the foreground and others in the back-ground, some dead, others wounded, and others again covered by mountains and the ruins of buildings. Wherefore let no one ever think to see any work of the brush more horrible and terrifying, or more natural than this one; and whoever enters that room and sees the windows, doors, and other suchlike things all awry and, as it were, on the point of collapse, and the mountains and buildings hurtling down, cannot but fear that everything will fall upon him, and, above all, as he sees the Gods in the Heaven rushing, some here, some there, and all in flight. And what is most marvellous in the work is to see that the whole of the painting has neither beginning nor end, but is so well joined and connected together, without any divisions or ornamental partitions, that the things which are near the buildings appear very large, and those in the distance, where the landscapes are, go on receding into infinity; whence that room, which is not more than 30 feet in length, has the appearance of open country. Moreover, the pavement being of small round stones set on edge, and the lower part of the upright walls being painted with similar stones, there is no sharp angle to be seen, and that level surface has the effect of a vast expanse, which was executed with much judgment and beautiful art by Giulio, to whom our crafts-men are much indebted for such inventions.

Most of the rest of Giulio Romano's work is also to be found in Mantua; in the Cathedral and the Palazzo Ducale and, above all, in his own house. This was built shortly before his death in 1546 and is important to us principally because there can be no question of any

108 Mantua, Palazzo Ducale, Cortile della Mostra, by Giulio Romano

109 Mantua, Giulio Romano's house, 1540s

outside pressure brought to bear on him. He was the favourite artist of the Duke and obviously, from the size of his house, fairly prosperous. The façade can best be described as a parody of Bramante's House of Raphael. The way in which the string-course is peaked up in the centre to form a sort of incomplete pediment, which in turn presses down on the keystone of the flattened arch below it, is quite obviously a deliberate reversal of Bramante's ideas. The same is true of the curious window frames forced into shallow arches which are slightly too small for them and surmounted by an elaborate entablature which has no columns to carry it. Such a solecism would have been unthinkable in the first years of the sixteenth century, but by the 1540s it could be considered witty and amusing. This alone will demonstrate the slightly precious quality of much of the best Mannerist architecture and is perhaps also an explanation of the fact that the style is more popular among architectural historians than with the general public.

[78]

160

CHAPTER EIGHT

Peruzzi and Antonio da Sangallo the Younger

Baldassare Peruzzi was, like Raphael and Giulio Romano, a leading member of the Bramante circle. He was a Sienese painter and architect, born in 1481, who came to Rome about 1503 and died there in 1536. According to the account given of him by Vasari he was most famous among his contemporaries as the man who revived the long-dead art of stage design and, connected with this, he was also a virtuoso in the art of perspective. Hundreds of his drawings still exist, mainly in Florence and Siena, but his personality remains somewhat mysterious. He is perhaps best remembered as Bramante's principal assistant, and was in his turn the master of Serlio. We know that Serlio in his treatise made extensive use of Peruzzi's drawings, and we know that both Bramante and Peruzzi projected treatises of their own which have not come down to us. Serlio's book, therefore, is an important source of information on both Peruzzi and Bramante, but, apart from this, we have a few paintings by Peruzzi and two buildings, both of which were attributed to him by Vasari.

The earlier of the two is the Villa Farnesina near the Tiber in Rome, begun in 1509 and completed in 1511. The building is comparatively small, but is nevertheless important as an early example of the villa type with a central block and projecting wings. It is much earlier than the Villa Madama and, indeed, at first glance it might well be taken for a fifteenth- rather than a sixteenth-century building. The patron was the Sienese banker Agostino Chigi, for whom Raphael was later to decorate the Chigi Chapel, and the purpose of the building seems to have been that of a *villa suburbana*. The exterior has had its effect much modified by the fact that the five bays on the ground floor of the entrance front have been glazed, so that the contrast of void and solid has been entirely done away with. The glazing was, however, necessary, since this entrance loggia contains a superb series of frescoes of Cupid and Psyche by Raphael and his pupils. For the rest, the façade has also been modified by the fact that the plain walls were originally decorated with frescoes which have long since weathered away. This explains the odd discrepancy between the bareness of the walls and

[110–12]

PALAZZO DE GHIGI ALLA LVNGARA ARCHITETTVRA DEL FAMOSISSIMO BALDASSARRE PERVZZI DA SIENA CHE FV ECELLENTE PITTOR E GIOMETRA L ANNO MDXVIII

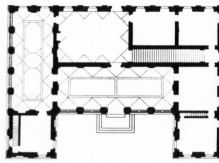

ROME,
VILLA FARNESINA
by Peruzzi, 1509–11

110 Engraving of
façade

111 Plan

112 Fresco in the
Sala delle Prospettive

the richness of the modelled frieze below the eaves, with its cherubs and swags pierced by small attic windows. The architecture is of a simplicity which recalls Francesco di Giorgio (who may well have been Peruzzi's master), and the uncomfortable effect of the central pilaster which divides the ends of the wings into two rather than three bays is one of the reasons for the slightly old-fashioned appearance of the building.

Peruzzi was also one of the numerous painters employed on the interior decoration, and we can understand his contemporaries' enthusiasm for his illusionistic skill as a stage designer when we see what he made of the big room on the first floor known as the Sala [112] delle Prospettive. The illusion of an opening, giving on to a view across Rome, is quite startlingly realistic.

For nine years after the completion of the Villa Farnesina Peruzzi worked, first with Bramante and then with Raphael, on St Peter's. There are scores of drawings by him, which pose numerous problems since it is impossible to be certain whose ideas they represent. In 1520, after Raphael's premature death, Peruzzi was appointed Head of the Works, but he accomplished very little, and in 1527 he was captured in the Sack of Rome which suspended all work on the building for many years. He was fortunate enough to escape to Siena, where he worked for some time before returning to Rome, where he was once more nominated as Capomaestro of St Peter's in 1530. But he did not settle in Rome until March 1535, and he died there on the 6th January of the following year.

This precision of dating is of some importance, since his last and greatest work, the palace which he built in Rome for the brothers [113–15] Pietro and Angelo Massimi, was certainly finished after Peruzzi's death and cannot have been begun before 1532, and possibly not until 1535. It is often regarded as an example of Early Mannerism and it is therefore important to notice that it dates from a later period than the Palazzo del Tè and Raphael's Roman palaces.

The Palazzo Massimi was built on the site of a palace belonging to the family, which had been burnt in the Sack. Some parts of the less-important buildings still stood and Peruzzi was commissioned to build two separate palaces for the two brothers on a single, irregular site, making use, as far as possible, of the surviving buildings. The plan is proof of his skill in arranging a large number of state rooms, [113] all of which are rectangular in shape, on a very awkward site, and with

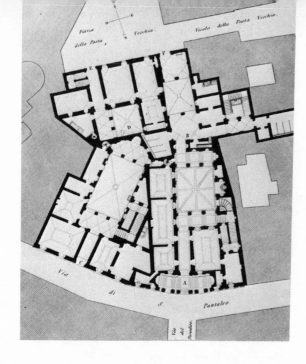

ROME, PALAZZO
MASSIMO ALLE COLONNE
by Peruzzi,
begun 1532/35

113 Plan

114 Façade

115 Court

an apparently symmetrical disposition about the main axes. It can be seen on plan that the axes are in fact slightly skewed, but this is not perceptible in the actual building. The palace on the right-hand side [114] of the plan, which has the grander façade, is that of Pietro Massimi, Angelo's palace, on the left, being simpler in construction. The plan also shows the feature, unique at this date, of a curved façade so as to make the fullest use of the site. It is very difficult to see the façade properly since it stands on a curve and opposite a T-junction in such a way that the spectator can hardly get far enough away to take in the building as a whole, which probably explains the difference in the treatment of the façades of the two palaces. The façade of the Palazzo Pietro Massimi is the one which is held to contain Mannerist elements. The disposition is roughly that of the Bramantesque type, a heavy basement with a *piano nobile* and attic floors above it separated by a strongly marked cornice. As in Raphael's Palazzo Branconio, however, the columns have been moved down to the ground floor instead of the first floor, and the rustication is now made to run the whole height of the building. Further, the columns are themselves arranged in an alternating rhythm so that there are bays with windows in them framed by two pilasters, followed by a bay with a pilaster

and a full column, and then, on the central axis in the entrance loggia, there are bays with pairs of full columns. The disposition as a whole is, however, strictly symmetrical. Above the cornice of the order there is a second band of stone which unites the projecting window sills, thus emphasizing the horizontal band which runs across the palace at about one-third of the whole height. What is, however, responsible for the rather beetling appearance of the façade is the fact that the mass of rusticated wall above this band is divided into three by the large windows of the *piano nobile* and then by two rows of attic windows of identical size. This break with the normal practice of diminishing the size of the windows in a regular order towards the roof means that the upper part of the palace has an uncomfortable air about it. The elaborate framework surrounding the attic windows was later to be developed by Serlio into the strapwork which spread like a rash all over northern Europe in the later sixteenth and early seventeenth centuries.

The main courts of both palaces are designed as a Roman atrium, partly no doubt because the Massimi flattered themselves that they were descended from the great Roman Fabius Maximus, and were therefore anxious that their palace should be as 'antique' as possible. The difficulties of arranging the court were met by Peruzzi with [115] great skill, since the photograph of the Palazzo Pietro Massimi shows the way in which the lower order has pierced vaulting above it which not only lights the internal loggia but which also greatly reduces the apparent discrepancy in height between it and the open loggia on the first floor. This trick of perspective, worthy of the painter of the Sala delle Prospettive, manages to persuade us that the two floors are visually equal. The first-floor loggia is very richly decorated, as befits the *piano nobile*.

The most important palace built in Rome at about the same time as Peruzzi's Palazzo Massimi was the gigantic Palazzo Farnese, by Antonio da Sangallo the Younger. He was the nephew of the architects Giuliano and Antonio da Sangallo the Elder and was trained by them before he went to Rome, at the age of twenty, about 1503. He died in Rome in 1546, having spent much of his life working on St Peter's; first as Bramante's assistant and draughtsman, and in the last years of his life in charge of the building and responsible for a great [90] wooden model which still survives. One of Antonio's earliest works

166

is the Palazzo Baldassini in Rome, of about 1503, which already shows his massive but rather unimaginative style. He was far less sensitive than Peruzzi, who must have worked in close contact with him under Bramante, but he had a great feeling, perhaps inherited from his uncle Antonio the Elder, for simple, massive masonry. At the same time his enthusiasm for ancient Roman architecture, though great, was not very profound and he tended to use motives from the Colosseum or the Theatre of Marcellus rather haphazardly. It was possibly this rather stodgy outlook which made him so disliked by Michelangelo. The difference between the two men can be seen not only in Michelangelo's drastic revision of Sangallo's work at St Peter's, but also in what is incontestably Antonio's masterpiece, the Palazzo Farnese.

Antonio entered the service of Cardinal Farnese quite early in his career and began a palace for him about 1513. Work proceeded very slowly, but when, in 1534, Cardinal Farnese became Paul III the whole plan was greatly enlarged and altered. The palace now became [116] the headquarters of the newly-rich and not very popular Farnese family and the vast design was carried on by Antonio until just before his death in 1546. The Pope held a competition for the design of the great crowning cornice; to Antonio's extreme mortification it was decided to use a design by Michelangelo. In fact, Michelangelo completed most of the palace immediately after Antonio's death, making a number of modifications to the original design.

The palace itself is by far the largest and most magnificent of all Roman princely palaces.[24] It occupies the whole of one side of a large [118] piazza and is conceived as a vast cliff-like block, the main front of which is nearly 100 feet high and nearly 200 feet long. The plan shows Florentine rather than Roman characteristics, since it consists of a free-standing block, roughly square in shape, arranged round a square central court. Most of the rear part of the palace, including the great open loggia with a view towards the Tiber, was completed at the end of the sixteenth century, but the main façade is far closer in spirit to the Palazzo Pitti in Florence than to Peruzzi's contemporary work at the Palazzo Massimi. There is no attempt at breaking up the vast extent of walling by means of a rusticated base with orders above it. As in the Florentine fifteenth-century example, the texture is obtained partly by rusticated quoins at the angles which gradually diminish upwards and by the placing and arrangement of the window openings. The floors are separated by strongly marked horizontal cornices and by bands of stone running above the window balconies at the level of the base of the small columns which frame each of the window openings. This type of tabernacle window set in a plain mass of masonry is due to Antonio da Sangallo, but on the main façade there are two characteristic touches by Michelangelo. One is the strongly projecting crowning cornice, which is very classical in detail and was raised some feet higher than Antonio da Sangallo had intended, in order to avoid the appearance of crushing the top storey. More typically Michelangelesque is the treatment of the great central window with the Farnese arms above it, immediately over the rusticated archway of the main entrance. In this case the main window is stressed by being reduced in size and apparently pushed deeper into the surface of the wall, a kind of inverted emphasis which, as we shall see, is very typical of Michelangelo's personal form of Mannerism.

[117] One enters the palace through a single arch which leads into a narrow but immensely impressive entrance tunnel with antique granite columns separating the central carriageway from the pavements on either side. This heavy classicism is certainly due to Antonio and is usually said to be derived from the Theatre of Marcellus. The court quite clearly derives from the Theatre of Marcellus and the

ROME,
PALAZZO FARNESE   by Antonio da Sangallo the Younger and Michelangelo,
begun 1513, enlarged 1534–46

116 Plan   117 Entrance vestibule

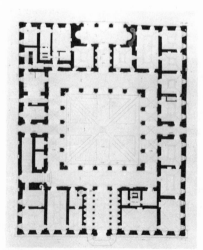

118 Façade

119 Reconstruction
of Sangallo's design   120 Court

Colosseum, since it consists of a series of superimposed arcades. It is also clear that the ground floor and the first floor are simply arcades which are certainly the work of Antonio da Sangallo, while the upper floor is neither simple nor an arcade; and in its extreme sophistication is just as typical of the work of Michelangelo. It seems most likely that Antonio's original design was for three arcades with the arches supported by the piers and with an attached order of Doric, Ionic, and Corinthian columns more or less as a decorative motive. At some point it became necessary to fill the arches of the two upper storeys and it is evident that the whole of the upper storey in its present form was designed and executed by Michelangelo. It is also probable that he designed the very unorthodox frieze above the Ionic order, as well as the window frames set into the filled arches of the first floor. It is possible to see in the actual building one or two places where balconies have been walled up and windows clearly inserted into what was originally an open arcade. The palace is, of course, both larger and more splendid than the Palazzo Massimi, but both show a deliberate intention on the part of the architect to re-create as far as possible a classical building. Peruzzi's is the more inventive, but Sangallo's is typical of an established, academic, type of architecture which, on account of its code of rules, could be taught. It was in fact a kind of grammar which lasted well into the nineteenth century, as may be seen in London buildings like the Reform Club in Pall Mall or the great Victorian town-houses in Kensington, where the tabernacle windows are the remote descendants of those in the Palazzo Farnese. This simple, rather unimaginative kind of architecture has much to recommend it as a basis of instruction and Antonio da Sangallo's memory is sometimes unjustly blamed for faults which were not his. Michelangelo disliked his fellow Florentine for a number of reasons, one being that he suspected Antonio of making a good thing out of the building of St Peter's; but he was also on firm ground when he attacked what he called the 'Sangallo gang' for their dullness and lack of imagination. It is precisely this imaginative quality which gives Michelangelo's own architecture its incontestable greatness but, at the same time, it was calculated to surprise and shock many of his contemporaries and perhaps even to lead some of them astray. Michelangelo as an architect was one of the inventors, and certainly the greatest exponent, of Mannerism, and his architectural works therefore deserve a chapter to themselves.

170

CHAPTER NINE

Michelangelo

Michelangelo Buonarroti was born in 1475 and died in 1564. In the course of this extremely long lifetime he established himself as incomparably the greatest artist in the world in painting, in sculpture, and in architecture. In addition to this, he also wrote some of the finest poems in the Italian language. His character was exceedingly difficult, yet he commanded an almost idolatrous veneration from practically all the younger artists of his day and his personal piety was such that it became a byword among his contemporaries; he was, for example, the friend of St Ignatius Loyola, the founder of the Society of Jesus. Although he always claimed to be a sculptor and nothing else, he soon found himself compelled to paint the vast fresco cycle on the vault of the Sistine Chapel, and, with the original designs for the projected monument to Julius II, he found himself involved in architectural activity. The perpetual postponement of the work on the tomb for Julius was effected by the Pope's successors by giving Michelangelo some other urgent commission which was to take precedence. One such commission was the work for the Medici family in Florence, which began with a projected façade for Brunelleschi's church of S. Lorenzo, was continued in the same church with the Medici Chapel or New Sacristy which balances Brunelleschi's Old Sacristy, and also included the building of the Biblioteca Laurenziana as part of the monastery of S. Lorenzo itself. Michelangelo's approach to these problems is best stated by Vasari, who claimed to have been taken as a fourteen-year-old boy to Florence in 1525 and placed with Michelangelo as a pupil. Many years later he described Michelangelo's work at S. Lorenzo in these words:

> And since he wished to make it in imitation of the Old Sacristy that Filippo Brunelleschi had built, but with another kind of ornament, he made a composite ornament, in a more varied and more original manner than any other master at any time, whether ancient or modern, had been able to achieve, for in the novelty of the beautiful cornices, capitals, bases, doors, tabernacles, and tombs, he made it very different from the work regulated by measure,

order, and rule, which other men did according to normal usage and following Vitruvius and the antiquities, to which he would not conform. That licence has done much to give courage to imitate him to those who have seen his methods, and new fantasies have since been seen which have more of the grotesque than of reason or rule in their ornaments. Therefore the craftsmen owe him an infinite and everlasting obligation, because he broke the bonds and chains of usage they had always followed. Afterwards he demonstrated his method even more clearly in the library of S. Lorenzo, at the same place; in the beautiful arrangement of the windows, in the pattern of the ceiling, and in the marvellous vestibule or *ricetto*. Nor was there ever seen a more determined grace of style, both in the whole and in the parts, as in the consoles, tabernacles, and cornices, nor any staircase more convenient; in which he made such bizarre breaks in the outlines of the steps, and departed so much from the common use of others, that everyone was amazed.

Michelangelo was first commissioned to add a façade to the church of S. Lorenzo in 1516. He wasted several years on the project – which eventually fell through – but it is reasonably well known to us from [121]   descriptions, drawings, and a wooden model. It is generally agreed that the wooden model does not represent Michelangelo's final design, but is basically representative of his intentions; and from it it is evident that he was designing a large frontispiece intended to carry a great deal of sculpture, rather than designing a façade which would express the shape of Brunelleschi's building in architectural terms. This conception of a building as an extension of sculpture is fundamental to Michelangelo's architecture and may be seen very clearly in the Medici Chapel of S. Lorenzo. The purpose of the chapel was to commemorate various members of the Medici family, and the design therefore sprang from an intention to provide a mausoleum or mortuary chapel. The design as a whole – which was never completed – takes on its full meaning only when we realize that the statues of the dead men, of the Medici patron saints, and of the Madonna and Child, [122]   and the architecture itself must all be read together, and are intended to be seen from a position behind the altar looking towards the far end of the Chapel where the Madonna statue was to be placed. The two executed tombs of Lorenzo and Giuliano de' Medici represent

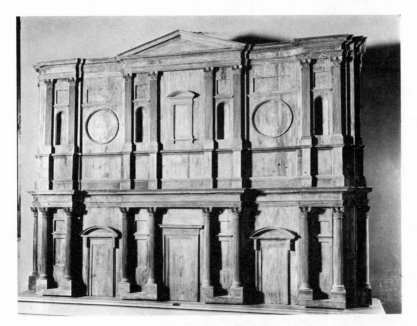

121 Florence, S. Lorenzo. Wooden model of the façade, attributed to
Michelangelo

the Contemplative and the Active Life respectively; and the contemplative figure of Lorenzo, with his head propped on his hand,
looks towards the Madonna as does the figure of Giuliano in his more
vigorous pose. The statues of both men are placed above symbolical
sarcophagi, each of which has two reclining statues. Those represent-
ing Dawn and Twilight accompany the figure of Lorenzo while the
more active states, symbolized by Day and Night, accompany the
tomb of Giuliano. In the original design there were to be two further [124]
figures reclining at floor level which would have helped to correct
the impression, given by the present arrangement, of the figures
sliding off the lids of the sarcophagi. It would also have resulted in
a powerful triangular composition, the apex of which would have
been formed by the figures of the dead Medici. The architectural
arrangement, with three vertical divisions of which the side bays have
blank niches with large segmental pediments above them, is concentrated on the figure in the central bay which receives a negative

173

122 View from the altar

123 Section

[124]   emphasis from the fact that it is closely framed by a pair of pilasters
but has no pediment to distinguish it. The niche itself, however, is
deeper than the empty niches at either side of it. This negative
emphasis is in itself a Mannerist characteristic, but Michelangelo's
importance as a creator of Mannerism can be still more clearly seen in
details such as the blind tabernacle over the doors. Here, at first sight,

174

124 Tomb of Giuliano de' Medici

we have a perfectly simple tabernacle frame surrounding a blank [122]
niche and itself framed by large Corinthian pilasters. In fact, we
notice that the pediment is very slightly too large for the space it
occupies so that it appears to be uncomfortably crushed by the
pilasters on either side. The space inside the tabernacle is still more
complicated. To begin with, the tabernacle itself apparently consists

175

of a segmental pediment supported by two pilasters, but the pilasters do not correspond to any of the classical orders and have curious sunk panels on their faces. The segmental pediment is apparently double at the top of the arch, where a second arc-like form is superimposed on the original pediment. Still more surprisingly, the bottom of the pediment is cut away and the niche appears to flow upwards into the pediment space, while at the bottom it is apparently forced outwards by the insertion of a meaningless block of marble. Finally, the flat wall of the niche is cut back in order to receive a patera and a richly carved swag. In short, the elements of the classical vocabulary have been somewhat brutally treated and recombined to give a series of forms which at that time were unique. As Vasari says, he 'made it very different from the work regulated by measure, order, and rule'. This work was designed some years before Giulio Romano's Palazzo del Tè and is, therefore, one of the first as well as one of the finest examples of Mannerism. We know that the planning of the Chapel began in November 1520, and was continued until 1527 when the Medici were expelled and, for a short time, Michelangelo was occupied in fortifying Florence for the Republican Government, which he himself supported. In 1530, however, work had to begin again since the Medici had been restored by force of arms and he found himself unable to resist their demands for a resumption of work. In 1534 Michelangelo finally left Florence and settled in Rome, leaving both the Medici Chapel and the Biblioteca Laurenziana incomplete. The Chapel has never been finished, but a part of the work on the Library was completed by Amannati. The work in the New Sacristy has an obvious reference to Brunelleschi's Old Sacristy, and in some ways is no more than a restatement of the Brunelleschian theme in terms of Michelangelo's own version of classic architecture [125, 126] at this stage of his career. The Biblioteca Laurenziana, however, was an entirely new creation, and in the vestibule Michelangelo's personal forms can be seen even more clearly than in the Medici Chapel. The commission seems to have been given in December 1523, or January 1524, and several alternative plans were submitted in 1524. The vestibule caused some difficulty because Michelangelo proposed to light it from the top; this was vetoed by Clement VII, the head of the Medici family, and in order to comply with the Pope's demands for windows in the side walls Michelangelo evolved the remarkable structure we now see. The floor level of the Library proper is

176

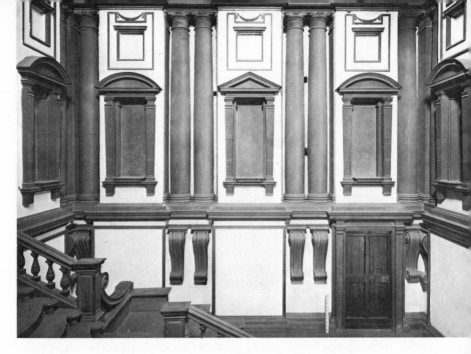

FLORENCE,
BIBLIOTECA LAURENZIANA
by Michelangelo, begun 1524

125 Vestibule, showing interior elevation

126 Vestibule staircase

considerably higher than that of the vestibule, since it is carried on piers over the top of the existing monastic buildings, another condition laid down by the Pope. It was also necessary to carry the walls of the vestibule upwards in order to insert the windows. The result is a unique room, very much higher than it is wide or long and with almost the entire floor-space occupied by a gigantic flight of steps, three flights wide at the bottom, which appears to flow down from the Library level spreading outwards over the floor of the vestibule like lava. The inside walls of the vestibule are treated like so many façades, as though they were turned inwards on themselves and enclosing the stairway. As in the Medici Chapel the tabernacle niches are distinctly odd in form, but the most striking feature of the vestibule as a whole is the way in which the columns are apparently sunk into the wall rather than standing away from it; they also appear to be supported by great pairs of console brackets. It has recently been shown that this curious treatment of the supporting columns, as though they were sunk back into the wall which they nominally support, is really in accordance with the structural facts of the building, since the Library was built on an existing foundation wall, which forms the only support for the columns. Nevertheless, the effect is very odd and has precisely that quality of unexpectedness which we associate with Mannerism and with Michelangelo: there can be no doubt that had Brunelleschi been faced with a similar problem he would have evolved some more straightforward solution. The stairway was completed in the 1550s by Vasari and Amannati jointly, but they do not seem entirely to have followed Michelangelo's original ideas, although he sent a small model from Rome in 1558/9.

Michelangelo spent the last thirty years of his life in Rome, where he began a number of major architectural commissions, although hardly any were executed entirely in accordance with his plans. By far the most important was the work done at St Peter's from 1546 until his death, which he regarded as the greatest work of his life, and for which he refused to take a salary.

Nevertheless, he began a number of other undertakings, some of which he supervised in considerable detail. The most important secular works undertaken in his last years were the redesigning of the Capitoline Hill in Rome and the fortified gateway known as the Porta Pia. The Capitol has always been the centre of the government of Rome and in the time of the Roman Republic and Empire it was often referred to as the centre of the world, *Caput Mundi*. The intention to replan the whole area and give it a more worthy setting was therefore a political undertaking of great importance, which began in 1538 with the transference there of the statue of Marcus Aurelius, the only equestrian statue of a Roman Emperor to come down untouched from the second century to the present time. It was believed in the Middle Ages and later that the Emperor was not Marcus Aurelius but Constantine, the first Christian Emperor, and the significance of the statue as a symbol of the Christian Empire was therefore of great importance in the redesigning of the Capitoline Hill. Michelangelo's designs began in 1546, but unfortunately the work was extremely slow and changes were introduced by Giacomo della Porta after Michelangelo's death. We have a series of engravings made within five years of Michelangelo's death which give a good idea of his intentions; from these it can be seen that he intended to enclose the whole space into a wedge-shaped plan with the wider end of the quadrilateral occupied by the Palace of the Senators, the actual seat of government of Rome, and with the shorter end opening on to the staircase which slopes sharply down the hillside. This trapezoidal form is emphasized by the oval pavement in the centre of the space, which in turn concentrates on the statue of Marcus Aurelius: della Porta's revision of the whole design modified Michelangelo's forms and changed the inward concentration into an expansion outwards by altering the design of the pavement and, above all, by substituting four streets opening off at the angles for the three projections on Michelangelo's plan. In recent years the pavement has been relaid according to Michelangelo's design but with della Porta's four streets left, so that the present position is even more confused than it was before. The palaces at either side of the open space, which now house two museums, were also altered by della Porta, but much of Michelangelo's original work remains and can be seen in a detail such as that shown in plate 130. From the point of view of architectural history the most important innovation made in these palaces was the introduction of the so-called Giant Order; that is, a pilaster or column which runs through two whole storeys.[25] Here the pilasters stand on high bases but they serve to tie together the two storeys of the building, the lower storey of which has another new motive in that the columns carry straight entablatures instead of arches. The relationship set up between the giant pilasters, the columns on the ground

[127–30]

[127]

179

MICHAELIS·ANGELI·BONAROTI·ARCHITECTVRA·ICHNOGRAPHIA
ROMAE·ANNO·ↀↀↃLXVII

ROME, CAPITOL
replanned by Michelangelo, 1546

127 Plan, with
Palazzo Capitolino on the left

128 Elevation of
Palazzo Capitolino

129 General view,
engraving by Dupérac

130 Detail of Palazzo Capitolino

floor, and the smaller columns of the tabernacle windows on the upper floor is thus extremely complex and very far removed from the simple proportions which would have been used by a fifteenth-century architect. Once again the details of the windows, or the panelling which apparently underlies the Giant Order, are characteristic of the Mannerist love of complexity.

Michelangelo's last works were the Sforza Chapel in the Early Christian basilica of Sta Maria Maggiore, a highly sophisticated essay in vaulting, and the fortified gate known as the Porta Pia. Most of the Porta Pia was executed after Michelangelo's death, but he made at least three drawings, and building began in 1562. The engraving of 1568 shows that, by comparison with the tabernacle in the Medici Chapel of some forty years earlier, Michelangelo's forms have become even more complicated; as for example the insertion of a broken segmental pediment inside an unbroken triangular one. At the same time, he shows great interest in contrasts of texture expressed in the smooth walling of the centre part and the rough stonework of the side bays. The inventive fantasy displayed in the window openings was to be taken up and carried still further by the architects of the seventeenth century, such as Bernini and Borromini, who were deeply indebted to Michelangelo's Roman works.

[131]

PORTAM·PIAM·A·MICHAELIS·ANGELI
BONAROTI·EXEMPLARI·ACCVRATISSIME
DELINEATAM·ROMA·CⅠƆ·Ɔ·LXVIII

131 Rome, Porta Pia,
by Michelangelo.
Begun 1562.
Engraving by E. Dupérac

CHAPTER TEN

Sanmicheli and Sansovino

Bramante's ideas received the widest dissemination in Italy because his very numerous pupils and assistants were scattered all over the peninsula, while the second generation – his pupils' pupils – often worked outside Italy or, as in the case of Serlio, wrote treatises which helped to spread Bramante's ideas. Giulio Romano, Raphael's pupil, had practised a very altered form of Bramante's classicism in Mantua, but the most important influence in the north of Italy came from Venetian territory where Sanmicheli and Sansovino were active in the second quarter of the sixteenth century. The great political crisis following the Sack of Rome in 1527 meant that almost no commissions were available in Central Italy but, on the other hand, the Venetian State remained powerful and required the services of military engineers as well as architects. Both Sanmicheli and Sansovino were salaried officials of the Venetian Republic, though only Sansovino did much work in Venice itself. Michele Sanmicheli (1484–1559) was born in Verona, which was then part of the Venetian territory. He went to Rome as a boy of sixteen and probably worked as a pupil or assistant of Antonio da Sangallo, although the surviving drawings attributed to him do not tell us very much. In 1509 he went to Orvieto where he worked for nearly twenty years, building some small chapels and houses in Orvieto itself and the splendid Cathedral of Montefiascone, which is about twenty miles from Orvieto. Soon after 1527 he returned to his native Verona and began a long career as a military architect in the service of the Venetian State, undertaking a number of long journeys to such places as Crete, Dalmatia, and Corfu, where the outposts of Venetian power were the principal bulwarks against the Turkish threat. He also built a great fort at the Lido near Venice and several fortified gateways in Verona and elsewhere. There can be little doubt that, in the dangerous political situation of the mid sixteenth century, this was the most important service he could render his country, and much of his life was devoted to it. For us, with a few exceptions such as the fortified gates of Verona, it was a waste of a great artist's time – but it left a mark

132 Verona, Porta Palio, by Sanmicheli. 1530s

[132]
on his architecture. A fortress must not only be strong; it must also look strong, and Sanmicheli's Porta Palio and Porta Nuova look impregnable, simply because of the carefully considered rustication, the banding of the columns, and the heavy keystones over the small arches. The Porta Palio has a rusticated outer layer cut back to reveal yet further rustication, giving an impression of rugged solidity which is deliberately contrasted with the open arcade on the inner, town, side. The outer side, exposed as it was to cannon-balls, is still treated with the greatest richness possible in the Doric order, so that Vasari could write of the Veronese gates: 'In these two gates it may truly be seen that the Venetian Senate made full use of the architect's powers and equalled the buildings and works of the ancient Romans.'

[133–36]
[133]
As a domestic architect he left three important palaces in Verona, all of which seem to date from the 1530s and present a problem in chronology. The earliest of these is the Palazzo Pompei which must have been begun about 1530. It is essentially a version of Bramante's House of Raphael but with a slightly richer texture in keeping with North Italian taste. It consists of seven bays with a main entrance in the central bay, which is slightly wider than the window bays on either side. The ends of the building are closed by a coupled column and pilaster so that the perfectly even articulation of the House of Raphael becomes, in the Palazzo Pompei, an even articulation with slight stresses on the centre and ends. This was probably due to the fact that the ground floor of the palace is a part of it and is not used for sub-letting as independent shops, which in turn means that the

184

windows are slightly smaller than was the case in the House of Raphael and the main entrance is correspondingly larger. The additional width of the central bay would be awkwardly evident if it were not counterbalanced by the emphasis placed on each of the end bays by the coupled column and pilaster.

This tendency to adapt the House of Raphael for new purposes can be seen very clearly also in Sanmicheli's Palazzo Canossa, where the [134, 135] plan shows a departure from the type of Roman palace in favour of a form more reminiscent of Peruzzi's Farnesina. The back of the palace goes down to the very swift-flowing Adige, so that a fourth wall is unnecessary, and there is a three-sided court with the river at the rear. In some ways the Palazzo Canossa recalls Giulio Romano's Palazzo del Tè, as for example in the triple arches of the main entrance and the mezzanine windows on the ground floor. This would seem to indicate that the palace must date from the later 1530s (it was under construction in 1537), and it is in any case further removed from the House of Raphael type, yet the façade as a whole shows the basic division into a rusticated basement and a smooth *piano nobile* with large windows separated by pairs of pilasters. The mezzanine windows of the ground floor are repeated in the upper storey, so that the problem of providing sufficient accommodation has been overcome at the expense of a certain amount of formal lucidity. The *piano nobile* has a complicated texture which owes a great deal to Bramante's Belvedere at the Vatican as well as to the House of Raphael. The façade is again closed at the ends by superimposed pilasters, but the rest of the façade is simply articulated by coupled pilasters and large round-headed windows. The windows, however, have a strongly projecting impost moulding continuing on either side as far as the pilasters, which are further linked by a flat panel-like shape running from the windows behind the pilasters and out again into the next window bay. This gives a marked horizontal stress and is very similar to the panelling forms Bramante used in the Belvedere. [81]

Neither the Pompei nor the Palazzo Canossa prepares one for Sanmicheli's third major work, the Palazzo Bevilacqua. This is very [136] difficult to date since it is usually held to be related to Sanmicheli's work at the Pellegrini Chapel which probably dates from the 1540s.[26] It is evident that the Palazzo Bevilacqua owes a great deal to Giulio Romano and to the new Mannerist ideas, since the façade is an extremely complex interplay of motifs some of which can be traced

185

directly back to Giulio Romano. In the first place, the texture of the whole is much richer than any other building of the period with the exceptions of Giulio's Palazzo del Tè, Raphael's Palazzo Branconio, and some contemporary work by Sansovino in Venice. The rusticated basement is not only heavily textured in the cutting but has an order of banded pilasters, and there are richly carved keystones in the window heads; the window and door openings themselves have an alternating rhythm of small and large bays giving an ABABA rhythm, which means that the bays of the *piano nobile* must themselves follow this narrow-wide-narrow pattern and cannot be of the identical sizes used by Bramante. This in turn has led to the adoption of a triumphal arch motive on the *piano nobile* so that there is a small arch with a mezzanine above it followed by a large arch and then another small window; but the extreme complication of this façade becomes evident when one analyses it in further detail. Not only is there an ABA rhythm of the bays but there are, as it were, counterpoints introduced by the small – and very Mannerist – pediments set above the smaller arches, which are alternately triangular and segmental. Thus the façade should really be read in its present form ABCBCBA, but this is predicated on the assumption that the original intention of the designer was to place the main entrance on the central axis and not, as it now appears, in the second bay at the left. It is often assumed that the palace is incomplete and that there should be eleven bays instead of the present seven. This, however,

VERONA, PALACES
BY SANMICHELI

133 Palazzo Pompei,
begun *c.* 1530

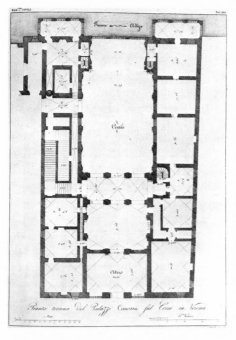

134, 135 Palazzo Canossa,
plan and façade, late 1530s

136 Palazzo Bevilacqua,
designed before 1537

is improbable since the palace is already large, and eleven bays would make it enormous for so comparatively modest a family; while the present 2:3 proportion of height to width also suggests completeness. Furthermore, there is a great complication introduced by the texture of the columns which separate the bays on the *piano nobile*. In the present building they are all fluted, and the order and entablature are correspondingly rich, but the flutings have a rhythm of their own which, starting at the left-hand corner of the palace, is straight, spiral to left, spiral to right, straight, straight, spiral to left, spiral to right, straight: that is to say, there is an ABCAABCA rhythm superimposed on the rhythm of the window bays, and in its present form the palace is symmetrical with the exception of the entrance bay which is off-centre.

In the smaller bays above the stilted pediments there are small mezzanine windows, while the spandrels of the large arches are filled with richly carved sculpture. The slightly uncomfortable feeling of the small mezzanine windows and the extreme richness of the sculpture and the cornice, as well as the rustication on the ground floor, have led many people to regard the Palazzo Bevilacqua as one of the great exemplars of Mannerism, but its genesis is perhaps even more interesting than one might infer from the influence of Giulio Romano. The heaviness of the rustication in the Porta Nuova or the Porta Palio is obviously intended to lend an air of strength, and it is likely that this feeling for light and shade, originally applied to military architecture, came to fascinate Sanmicheli for its own sake. Perhaps even more important is the fact that Verona is rich in classical remains and many of the motives on the Palazzo Bevilacqua, which occur with even greater richness in the Pellegrini Chapel, can be traced back to a desire to emulate antiquity. In fact, the plan of the Pellegrini Chapel is almost literally derived from the Pantheon in Rome, so that there can be no doubt that Sanmicheli was consciously emulating one of the great classical prototypes. This can be confirmed in the most striking way by walking fifty yards down the street from the Palazzo Bevilacqua to the great surviving Roman monument, the Porta de' Borsari, which is undoubtedly a Roman monument, although its exact date is disputed by archaeologists. It is, however, the source for the small stilted pediments, the spiral-fluted columns, and the general richness of effect of the Palazzo Bevilacqua; and it serves once more to show that the generation after Bramante had as

[*137, 143*]

188

passionate an interest in the remains of classical antiquity, but that their interest was concentrated on the later and richer Roman buildings. Perhaps this is most clearly seen in the work of Sanmicheli, but it can be paralleled in the works of his contemporary, the Florentine architect Jacopo Sansovino, who settled in Rome at about the same time as Sanmicheli and, like him, worked for the Venetian State from 1527 onwards.

Jacopo Sansovino was born in 1486 and died in 1570. He was originally a sculptor and was trained under Andrea Sansovino, from whom he took his own name. During his very long life he practised both as a sculptor and as an architect and we are comparatively well informed about him since he was a Florentine who made good in Venice and was thus the subject of a full account in Vasari's Lives, published in 1568. After Sansovino's death in 1570 Vasari revised the original life.[27] Sansovino's fame in Venice led to his friendship with great artists like Titian and Tintoretto, and the writer Pietro Aretino. Sansovino's own son was a writer of distinction and the author of one of the best Venetian guide-books, in which his father's works receive adequate attention. Sansovino, like Sanmicheli, was formed by Bramante and would have thought of himself as an essentially classical architect. He went to Rome in 1505/6 with Giuliano da

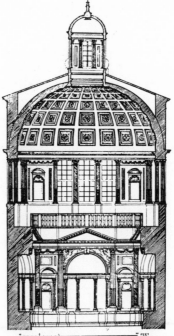

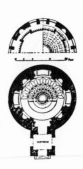

137 Verona,
Cappella Pellegrini.
Section and plan,
by Sanmicheli. 1529 and later

Sangallo and thus came into the Bramantesque circle at about the same time as Sanmicheli. For the next twenty-odd years he worked in Florence and in Rome where he began to practise as an architect after 1518. Like Sanmicheli he fled north in 1527 and spent the rest of his life in Venice. He again practised both as a sculptor and as an architect and his most famous statues, the *Mars* and the *Neptune*, are the gigantic figures which symbolize Venetian power on land and sea, standing at the head of the Scala dei Giganti in the Doges' Palace. They date from the end of his career, but they show very clearly a combination of the influence of Michelangelo with the study of classical sculpture and they can be taken therefore as typical of his aims in architecture. His earliest works in Venice were small jobs for the State until in 1529 he was appointed Principal Architect to the City. Much of his time was spent as the head of a department in improving the city, regulating markets, and similar work, but he held office for nearly forty years and during that time most of his greatest work was erected. His masterpiece is undoubtedly the great [138–40] Library which occupies one side of the Piazzetta of St Mark's facing the Doges' Palace. This library was originally founded by Cardinal Bessarion, who gave it as a token of gratitude to Venice in 1468. After long deliberation it was decided to erect a grand building to house the books and in 1537 Sansovino began work. The Library was completed, after his death, by Vincenzo Scamozzi between 1583 and 1588. The Library of St Mark's is frequently known as the Libreria Sansoviniana and is thus one of the very few buildings in the world to be known by the name of its architect. It has always enjoyed great fame and Palladio himself in 1570 refers to it as 'the richest and most ornate building that has been put up, perhaps since the time of the ancients' and he also paid it the compliment of imitating it very closely in his own Basilica at Vicenza. Nevertheless, on 18 December 1545 there was a heavy frost which caused part of the vaulting to fall in, and Sansovino was promptly thrown into prison from which he was rescued only by the intervention on his behalf of Aretino, Titian, and the Ambassador of the Emperor Charles V.

[140]   The air view shows more clearly than a normal view the complexity of the problem which faced Sansovino. He had in effect to design a building facing both St Mark's and the Doges' Palace which should stand up to both, but at the same time should not clash unduly with

either or minimize their importance as the two major buildings of the Republic. He also had to arrange his library in such a way that it forms the essential part of the Piazzetta and Piazza di San Marco, the only really large open space in Venice. Sansovino's solution depends on a very long unbroken façade which runs parallel to the long façade of the Doges' Palace and which, like it, has a matching return façade on the water's edge. By keeping the roof line lower than that of the palace Sansovino avoids dominating the scene, but by using a great deal of decorative sculpture and an extremely rich texture of light and shade he succeeds in holding his own with the richness and colour of St Mark's and the Doges' Palace. The detail shows how very much richer Sansovino's work is than would have been the case had Bramante been the architect, but the heaviness of the Doric order and the reference back to a classical prototype – the Theatre of Marcellus – are both entirely Bramantesque in feeling. We know from a contemporary dispute over the details of the Doric order that Sansovino's building was regarded as a model of correctness and it is evident that classical regularity was his principal aim. There is an obscure passage in Vitruvius in which he states that in a Doric temple there should be a half-metope[28] at the angle, and this is extremely difficult to arrange. What Sansovino did was to add heavy piers at the actual angles so that by making his metopes very slightly wider than was usual and adjusting the pier width to suit it the correct effect is obtained. This ingenious solution satisfied everybody, although it is in fact an evasion of the problem, since the piers can be made almost any width the architect desires. Nevertheless, the effect of the whole building is largely dependent on this, since it means that the frieze is rather too large, and the Doric order set against the arches is therefore different in proportion from that in the Palazzo Farnese, although both clearly derive from the same antique prototype. Again, Sansovino has taken great liberties with the upper part of the building, since the *piano nobile* has an Ionic order and is therefore taller than the ground-floor portico. The portico in fact is not really a part of the building at all since it was intended as a shelter for pedestrians and is now largely blocked by café tables. The Library proper is on the first floor and the difference in proportion is taken up by the smaller arches of the Library windows being supported on a separate, smaller, order. These smaller Ionic columns are fluted so that they will not clash too obviously with the larger, smooth ones next to them. Above the larger order is a very rich entablature with an elaborate carved frieze very high in proportion to the order below it and pierced by attic windows.

[139]   The total effect is thus one of great simplicity since the arches repeat down the very long façade to the Piazzetta, but at the same time the surface texture and the contrast of light and shade are as rich as possible. The use of the small columns on the first-floor windows reminds one of the so-called Palladian motive, and it is instructive to compare the treatment of this window with Palladio's

[162]   own version in his Basilica at Vicenza which dates from ten or a dozen years later. The interior of the Library has the same richness and elaboration although, like the outside, there is practically nothing which could be confused with the contemporary Mannerism of Giulio Romano.

    Sansovino's other major works in Venice were all begun at about the same time, and two of them are immediately next to the Library. In 1537 he began work on the Mint, which adjoins the Library on the waterfront; on the Loggia at the base of the Campanile of St Mark's, which stands at the opposite end of the Piazzetta; and on the great palace for the Cornaro family, the Palazzo Corner della Ca' Grande.

[139]   The Loggia of the Campanile was intended to harmonize the vertical shaft of the tower with the very long horizontal of the Library, so Sansovino adapted a single arcade form with an attic above it, which was divided into panels and ornamented with reliefs. He uses a triumphal arch rhythm with niches containing statues, so that the whole is reminiscent of the Library façade, but even more richly decorated. The present Loggetta dates from 1902, when it was reconstructed after the fall of the Campanile. At the opposite

[141]   end of the Library Sansovino built the Mint (la Zecca), which was originally only two storeys high. Its purpose was to hold the bullion reserves of the Republic and it is therefore a building which both looks and is extremely strong. It was finished by 1545 and Vasari says that it was Sansovino's first public building in Venice, by which he probably means that it was the first to be completed. He says further that Sansovino introduced the 'Rustic Order' into Venice in this building, and it is certainly true that the heavy, banded columns are reminiscent of the Palazzo del Tè and look forward to the great popularity of rusticated columns all over Europe in the later sixteenth and early seventeenth centuries. The introduction of this order into

192

VENICE, THE LIBRARY
(Biblioteca Marciana) by Sansovino,
begun 1537

138 Side facing the lagoon (Sansovino's Mint
on the left)

139 Façade facing the Doges' Palace (Sansovino's Loggia at the base of the Campanile on
the right)

140 Air view showing the Mint, Library,
Campanile, St Mark's and the Doges' Palace

northern Europe is due to the textbook of Sebastiano Serlio – and Serlio lived for several years in Venice.

[*142*]   The only major building by Sansovino in Venice which was commissioned by a private family is the Palazzo Corner, of which the foundation-stone was laid in 1537 and which was perhaps not finished until after Sansovino's death. This palace is the culmination of a long sequence of attempts to regularize the Venetian palace type of which the Palazzo Vendramin-Calergi was a good example. In the Palazzo Corner Sansovino has taken the rusticated basement of the House of Raphael type and combined it with the great triple-arched entrance of the Palazzo del Tè. As in earlier examples, the ground floor has small windows with mezzanines above and then the *piano nobile* and the floor above it are treated identically. Here the outer windows are placed between paired half-columns with a very small space between the window jamb and the column so that the three windows in the centre of the façade which light the *Gran Salone* are almost indistinguishable from the two pairs of windows on either side of them. On the other hand, the side windows have individual balconies while the *Gran Salone* has a single long balcony for all three windows, thus emphasizing the traditional central grouping at the same time as the architect is regularizing the façade as a whole. This palace became a standard type and later examples, such as the Palazzo Pesaro and the Palazzo Rezzonico, by Baldassare Longhena, in the late seventeenth century, are clearly derived from it. Sansovino is thus a characteristic sixteenth-century Venetian artist, like his friend Titian, aware of contemporary developments but very little affected by the more esoteric aspects of Mannerism.

141 Venice, la Zecca (the Mint), by Sansovino. Begun 1537

142 Venice, Palazzo Corner della Ca' Grande by Sansovino. Begun 1537

CHAPTER ELEVEN

Serlio, Vignola, and the late sixteenth century

The second half of the sixteenth century saw a great deal of architectural activity and was also a time when rules were formulated and
the architectural profession began to come into being. Most of the
later generation of Mannerists set great store by classical antiquity,
and by a knowledge of the rules which could be deduced from the
somewhat obscure writings of Vitruvius as well as from the remains
of ancient buildings. The earliest printed edition of Vitruvius dates
from about 1486 – about thirty years after the invention of printing.
The next half-century saw a number of editions both in Latin and in
Italian, with commentary and illustrations: the first Italian translation,
of 1521, was made by Cesariano, a pupil of Bramante. Practically all
the early editions were superseded in 1556 by Bishop Barbaro's,
which has illustrations by Palladio. Sixteenth-century architectural
treatises almost all depend on Vitruvius and therefore to some extent
on Alberti's interpretation of the Vitruvian rules as well, but the
three most important treatises, by Serlio, Vignola, and Palladio
himself, are all much more than mere derivations from Vitruvius.

Sebastiano Serlio was a Bolognese painter who was a contemporary
of Michelangelo (being born in 1475) and was therefore older than
Peruzzi, who seems nevertheless to have been his master. Serlio went
to France in 1541 and died there in 1554 (or just possibly 1555). He
began life as a painter, an expert in perspective, and was associated
with Peruzzi in Rome from about 1514 until the Sack, when he fled
to Venice and worked there for some years. Peruzzi bequeathed his
drawings to Serlio and it is possible that they included some by
Bramante himself, since Serlio seems to have had a first-hand
knowledge of some of Bramante's projects. It was not until he was
sixty-two, in 1537, that Serlio achieved anything of real importance.
In that year he published a prospectus for a treatise on architecture
in seven books, and, at the same time, he published Book IV of the
projected treatise under the title *Regole generali di architettura . . .
sopra le cinque maniere degli edifici . . . con gli esempi delle antichità, che
per la maggior parte concordano con la dottrina di Vitruvio*. The treatise

is a bibliographical muddle since it was published very irregularly:

[143] Book III, which deals with the antiquities of Rome, came out in Venice in 1540, while Books I and II came out as a single volume on geometry and perspective in 1545. They were published in France, as were also Book V, on churches, of 1547, and an additional book

[144] on various types of elaborate gateway published in 1551. This is known as the *Libro Extraordinario* and is often confused with Book VI which was never published in Serlio's lifetime, although manuscripts exist.[29] Book VII was published posthumously in Frankfurt in 1575 from Serlio's papers, and the manuscript of an eighth book has now been published. The treatise was immediately popular and was reprinted in Italian and in French on many occasions, while there were very soon translations, of the whole or parts, into Flemish, German, Spanish, and Dutch, and an English translation was made from the Dutch edition in 1611. The reason for this great popularity is that the treatise was not merely an exercise in Vitruvian theory; it was the first really practical handbook on the art of architecture. It was of immense importance in the history of European architecture, especially in France and in England, because it appeared to give a simple account of the elements of antique and modern architecture

143, 144 Plates from Serlio's *Architettura*. Plan of the Pantheon (from Book III, 1540), and Design for a Gateway, from the *Libro Extraordinario*, 1551

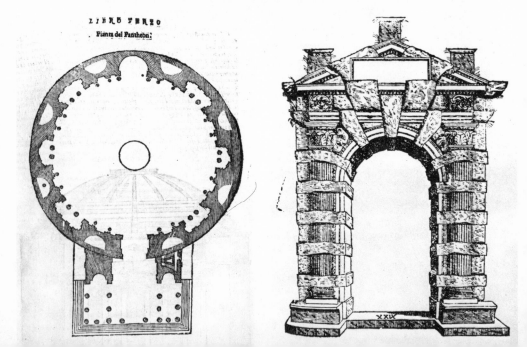

and was available in the vernacular. Perhaps the most important part was the illustrations, for Serlio seems to have been the inventor of the illustrated book in the sense in which the text merely elucidates the illustrations rather than the other way round. The fourth book, of 1537, deals with the classical orders by means of a series of simple diagrams and a text which explains how to construct each separate order. For this reason it was a best-seller and Serlio was able to present a copy to François I, which in due course led to his going to France, in 1541, as painter and architect to the King. The rest of his life was spent there, but almost nothing survives of his work, although the later books of the treatise show that his own not very pure Italian taste became progressively modified by French influence so that the later books, and particularly the *Libro Extraordinario*, are very far removed from the severe simplicity of Bramante, although they appealed at once to the unrefined tastes of English, Flemish, and French master-masons. The books themselves show quite clearly how a gentleman desiring to build could, by consulting his mason with a copy of Serlio, act as his own architect, for in Book III he could find fairly accurate representations of the better-known antiquities; from Book IV he could learn how to set out the orders; and from Book V he could learn about centrally planned churches, while from the other books he could obtain a whole grammar of ornament. Serlio's influence on both French and English architecture was in some ways disastrous, since master-masons tended to seize upon the more flamboyantly Mannerist features and to superimpose them on a fundamentally Gothic structure so that in England, at any rate, the classical phase did not come until after Serlio had been digested, and had to wait for Inigo Jones in the early seventeenth century. Jones himself derived most of his knowledge of good Italian building from another treatise, that by Palladio.

The third of the great treatise writers was Giacomo Barozzi da Vignola, who was born in 1507 and died in 1573. He was fifty-seven years old when Michelangelo died, but his career illustrates the apparent rigidity of Mannerist art in the second half of the sixteenth century; for many people felt that Michelangelo, though himself incontestably a great architect, was responsible for a great deal of fantasy and licence, and Vignola's successful career demonstrates the importance of correctness in the architecture of the third quarter of the sixteenth century. He was principally important as the designer

197

of two new types of church at the moment of the most active expansion of church building following the Counter-Reformation. In particular, Vignola's design of the Gesù, the mother church of the Society of Jesus, meant that copies of his design were carried all over the earth by Jesuit missionaries, and Vignola's architectural ideas may now be found from Birmingham to Hong Kong. Vignola was born in the small town of that name near Modena and began his career by drawing the antiquities in Rome in the mid 1530s; thus he did not arrive in Rome until the last years of Peruzzi's life, although his sober classicism derives through Peruzzi from Bramante. He went to France for eighteen months in 1541–3 where he met his fellow Bolognese, Serlio, and it was not until his return to Italy that he [182–85] began to build on his own account. The first of his major works was the villa (now in Rome), built for Pope Julius III from 1550, which is, in effect, the Belvedere of Julius III as against Bramante's Belvedere for Julius II. The Villa Giulia and the vast palace for the Farnese family at Caprarola, near Viterbo, were Vignola's major works in secular architecture and must be deferred to another chapter, where they can be seen along with other villas and palaces. His work for [145, 146] Julius III secured him the commission for the little church of S. Andrea in Via Flaminia. This was completed in 1554 and is the earliest of the three important churches built by Vignola. The small church, now rapidly falling into ruin,[30] is the earliest example of a church with an oval dome, a type that was to become popular during the seventeenth century. It derives from Roman tombs, the most famous example being that of Cecilia Metella; what Vignola has done is to take a square plan with a circular dome over it and to extend it along one axis, thus obtaining something which may be called an extended central plan. The interior of the church, with its very simple and austere panelling, shows quite clearly how the plan began as a square and circle and finished as a rectangle with an oval dome over it. The next step is obviously to extend the oval shape to the ground-plan itself, and this was done at the very end of Vignola's life in the small church in the Vatican (now usually inaccessible) of S. Anna [147] dei Palafrenieri. The church was begun in 1572/3 and was completed by Vignola's son. As may be seen from the plan, the façade was still flat although the oval dome was expressed internally on plan. Several later sixteenth-century and early seventeenth-century Roman churches descend directly from this earliest oval church.

198

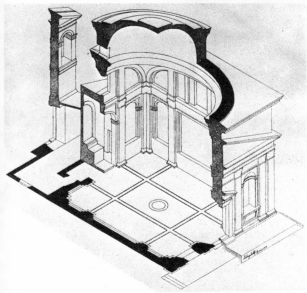

145, 146 Rome, S. Andrea in Via
Flaminia, finished 1554. Exterior
and diagram of construction

147 Rome, S. Anna dei
Palafrenieri, begun 1572/3.
Plan

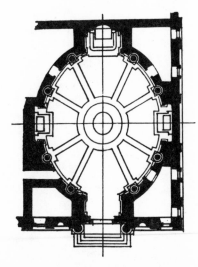

By far the most influential of Vignola's churches was the Gesù, although it was architecturally less adventurous. The Society of Jesus was founded in 1540 by St Ignatius Loyola, who was a friend of Michelangelo. The original plans of 1554 were made by Michelangelo himself but the church was not begun until 1568; it was then designed to seat a large congregation, all of whom would be able to hear the sermons that were so important a feature in Counter-Reformation religious life. A letter from Cardinal Farnese to Vignola, dated August 1568, stresses the importance of preaching, so that Vignola began the commission knowing that he would have to provide a building with a wide nave and a barrel-vault for acoustic reasons.

The letter says:

Father Polanco has been here, sent by the General of the Jesuits, and has been discussing with me some ideas concerning the building of the church. . . . You are to keep a watchful eye on the cost, which is not to exceed 25,000 ducats, and, within that limit, the church is to be well proportioned in length, breadth, and height, according to the rules of architecture. The church is not to have a nave and two aisles, but is to consist of one single nave, with chapels down each side. . . . The nave is to be vaulted, and is not to be roofed in any other way, in spite of any objections they may raise, saying that the voice of the preacher will be lost because of the echo. They think that this vault will cause the echo to resound, more than is the case with an open timber roof, but I do not believe this, since there are plenty of churches with vaults, of even bigger capacity, which are well adapted to the voice. In any case, you are to observe the points I have raised – namely, cost, proportion, site, and vaulted roof: as for the form itself, I depend on your judgement, and on your return you can give me an account, when you have agreed with all the other people concerned, after which I will make up my own mind, to which opinion you will all conform. Farewell.

[148, 32] The plan, with its side chapels instead of aisles, is obviously derived from the type established by Alberti in S. Andrea at Mantua; but the Gesù has a much wider and shorter nave as well as very shallow transepts. The shape of the nave is designed for audibility, while the east end with the great dome over the crossing allows a flood of light to fall on the High Altar and on the altars in each of the transepts,

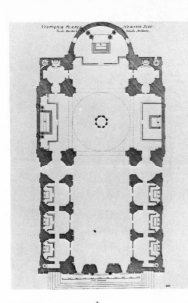

ROME, IL GESÙ
by Vignola,
finished by Giacomo della Porta

148 Plan
149 Vignola's design for the façade
150 Façade as built by della Porta

151 Rome, Il Gesù.
Painting by Sacchi
and Miel, showing
the original interior

[151]

[149–150]

[28]

dedicated to St Ignatius himself and St Francis Xavier, the first of many saints produced by the Society. The interior is almost entirely of the later seventeenth and nineteenth centuries and gives a completely wrong impression of the original design, which was austere in the extreme. Vignola died in 1573, when cornice level had been reached, and the façade has also been altered considerably from that which he originally intended. The present façade, by Giacomo della Porta, is less satisfactory than Vignola's two-storey design, with its emphasis on the vertical central element. This type of two-storey design with scrolls at the sides, like the plan of the Gesù, also derives from Alberti, in this case from his Sta Maria Novella in Florence. The influence of Vignola's Gesù has been such that it became almost the standard type of church plan and church façade.

202

In 1562 Vignola published his own treatise, entitled *Regola delli Cinque Ordini d'Architettura*, in obvious imitation of Serlio. His treatise is far more scholarly than Serlio's and has much better engravings: on the other hand, it deals only with the details of the classical orders and does not cover anything like the ground covered by Serlio. Nevertheless, it was the standard textbook for architectural students, particularly in France, for about three centuries and nearly two hundred editions of it are known. Towards the end of his life Vignola built an impressive gateway for the Farnese Gardens in [152] Rome, and this gives a very good idea of the precision with which he handled the classical orders. The gateway was demolished in 1880, but the stones were preserved and it has recently been re-erected in Rome.

The later sixteenth century saw a great wave of church building in Rome itself, and a few examples may be quoted to show how important Vignola's designs were. In the middle of the century there was a brief moment when the more fantastic aspect of Michelangelo's style seemed as though it might be continued by two men, Giacomo del Duca and Giacomo della Porta. Giacomo della Porta soon came under the influence of Vignola and evolved a rather dry classical style, lacking the imagination of Michelangelo and the precision of Vignola. Giacomo del Duca is a mysterious figure, who seems to have been a Sicilian. He was born about 1520, probably in Messina, and died at a great age, at some date after 1601, in Sicily. Most of his work seems to have been done in and around Messina and was

152 Rome, Orti Farnesiani.
Reconstruction of the original gateway by Vignola

thus destroyed in the great earthquakes. The small church of Sta Maria di Loreto in Rome gives an idea of his highly personal style. It was originally begun by Antonio da Sangallo the Younger and was taken over by Giacomo del Duca about 1577. He broke into the pediment of the Sangallo church and inserted a large window with a drum and dome above it, so that the whole upper part is disproportionately large. The details show the derivation of his forms from Michelangelo, and, in some ways – such as the huge ribs and the projection of the columns outside the ring at the top of the dome – it may be argued that Giacomo was even more licentious than Michelangelo himself. This type of Mannerism did not prove popular for churches and the more typical forms are those derived from or close to Vignola's. The church of Sto Spirito in Sassia, built by Antonio da Sangallo the Younger in the 1530s, has a two-storey façade which is probably the starting-point for Vignola's Gesù, as

it is certainly the starting-point for the façade of Sta Caterina dei Funari which, rather unusually, is signed and dated by the obscure architect Guidetti in 1564. This precedes Vignola's design for the façade of the Gesù, but it is clear that the two have much in common.[31]

After the death of Vignola in 1573 and before the rise of the great architects of the Early Baroque, the architectural scene in Rome was dominated by Giacomo della Porta, who was the official 'Architect to the Roman People', and by Domenico Fontana, the favourite architect of Sixtus V. As we have already seen, the two men collaborated on the completion of the dome of St Peter's. Neither was an architect of the first rank, but Fontana was the most skilful engineer of his generation and Giacomo della Porta was probably the most employed architect in Rome, with a hand in almost every major undertaking. His style can be seen very clearly in such works as the façade of the Gesù, as it actually exists, and from a building

such as the national church of the Greeks in Rome, S. Atanasio dei Greci, which is important in that the towers closing the façade look forward to the types developed in the seventeenth century, as for example in Borromini's S. Agnese and, ultimately, Wren's St Paul's.

Both della Porta and Fontana were employed by Pope Sixtus V (1585–90), and Fontana and Sixtus between them determined the layout of Rome for centuries to come. Rome, as it existed until the

1950s, was very largely a seventeenth-century city built on the layout which Sixtus imposed on it in the five years of his reign.

MANNERISM IN ROME

153 Sta Maria di Loreto,
begun by Antonio da
Sangallo the Younger; dome
by Giacomo del Duca, *c.* 1577

154 S. Atanasio dei Greci,
by Giacomo della Porta.
Elevation of façade

155 Sta Caterina dei Funari,
by Guidetti, 1564

FACIES EXTERNA TEMPLI SANCTI ATHANASII A GREGORIO. XIII.
PONT. OPT. MAX. GRÆCORUM NATIONI
EXÆDIFICATI.
Martino Longo Senese Architetto

Sixtus V was one of the most remarkable popes of the sixteenth century. He was a son of a gardener and began life as a shepherd and watchman. He became a Franciscan and his enormous energy and powers of administration made him General of his Order and finally Pope. In Domenico Fontana he found a similar type of practical man and between them they set about transforming Rome. In 1585 Fontana made his name by transporting the obelisk which had stood since classical times at one side of St Peter's to its present position in front of the church. This huge granite obelisk was raised vertically, lowered on to rollers, pulled round to the piazza and re-erected there; a feat of engineering which amazed his contemporaries. He was ennobled immediately, and later wrote a book about the whole undertaking. After this he put up several other obelisks for Sixtus V, who liked to erect them at the junctions of the great streets which he planned right across Rome. Between them they brought extra water – the Acqua Felice named after the Pope – to Rome, which led to the building of whole new quarters, as well as the provision of those fountains so typical of Rome. They also had some less praiseworthy ideas, such as the plan (fortunately never put into execution) to transform the Colosseum into a wool factory.

Most of the Vatican Palace as it exists today, and also most of the Lateran Palace, are by Fontana but neither is architecturally significant.[32] After the death of his great patron Fontana went to Naples, where he died in 1607. He was the uncle of Carlo Maderno and was, therefore, the founder of one of the great dynasties of Baroque architects.

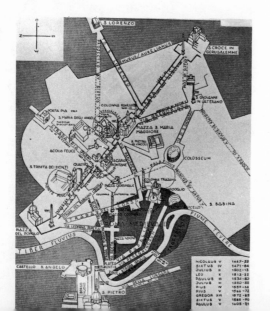

156 Rome. The town-planning projects of Sixtus V (reconstruction by S. Giedion)

CHAPTER TWELVE

Florentine Mannerists: Palladio

The greatest architect active outside Rome in the later sixteenth century was Andrea Palladio, but many other able men were then at work in Italy and three of them – Amannati, Buontalenti, and Vasari – must be noticed briefly. They represent Mannerist architecture in Florence and, as might be expected, they show the profound influence of Michelangelo, although the most important, Amannati, was also much influenced by the more classical styles of Vignola and Sansovino. He was born near Florence in 1511 and died there in 1592. As a boy he saw Michelangelo's New Sacristy being built, but he soon went to Venice and worked under Sansovino; like Sansovino, he practised both as a sculptor and as an architect. In 1550 he was in Rome where he began to work on the Villa Giulia   [183] with Vignola and Vasari, so that for the five years (1550–5) of Julius III's reign he was influenced by the architectural ideas of Vignola. On his return to Florence in 1555 he began to work for the Medici Duke, later the Grand Duke Cosimo I, often in collaboration with Vasari. His most important work was the extension and alteration of the Palazzo Pitti from about 1558 to 1570. Cosimo bought the Palazzo Pitti in 1549 with his wife's dowry, and from 1550 he planned to extend it and to lay out the splendid gardens in a manner befitting his new rank. Most of the original street front is now incorporated in the seventeenth-century additions, but Amannati is usually credited with the vast wings at the back, and the extension   [157] of the whole in an overwhelmingly grandiose rusticated form. The rusticated order in the court and the effect of texture seen from the gardens are perhaps the most striking aspects of Amannati's style, and it can clearly be seen that his bold handling of rustication owes much to Sansovino's Mint in Venice. His best-known building is   [141] probably the bridge over the Arno, the Ponte SS. Trinita, which had been destroyed by a flood and was rebuilt by Amannati in 1566–9 with the famous and very graceful flat arches. The bridge was wantonly destroyed in 1944 but has since been reconstructed. Amannati built some palaces in Florence and he also worked for the Florentine State outside the city, as for example at Lucca, where he probably built most of the Palazzo della Signoria. It is known that his design was accepted in 1577, but there is a letter from him to the Town Council explaining that he is having trouble with his eyes, and probably towards the end of his life he was able to work less and less. In 1582 he wrote the celebrated letter to the Academy which is one of the documents of the effect of Counter-Reformation ideas on aesthetics. This letter (which reads very like a sermon) is probably due to the fact that in his later years he had strong connections with the Jesuits. He claims, for example, that nude figures can be occasions of sin and he says that he wishes that some of his own works could be destroyed; he specifically mentions the very beautiful Neptune Fountain which he made for the Piazza della Signoria between 1563 and 1575. He claims that draped figures can show off the sculptor's skill just as well and he instances Michelangelo's *Moses* as his finest work: this is particularly revealing of the Mannerist tendency to exalt virtuosity above all other qualities. Another passage in the letter is interesting in that he says that most patrons accept what they get, rather than lay down strict instructions for the artist: 'Yet we all know that the majority of people who order works of art do not set any subject but leave it to our judgement, simply saying "here I want a garden, a fountain, a pool", and expressions of that sort.'

Giorgio Vasari was born in the same year as Amannati (1511) and died in 1574. He is, of course, immortal on account of his *Lives of the Most Illustrious Painters, Sculptors and Architects*, first published in 1550 and republished with extensive alterations and additions in 1568. In his own day he was also famous as a painter, architect, and general artistic impresario. As a painter he was more expeditious than skilful, but as an architect he left at least three notable works. In 1550 he helped to collaborate with Vignola and Amannati on the design of the Villa Giulia, but it is likely that his activity was almost entirely administrative. In 1554, however, he built the church of Sta Maria Nuova near Cortona and from 1560 until his death in 1574 he worked on the Palace of the Uffizi for Cosimo I in Florence. This building, which is now the famous picture-gallery, was designed as the government offices (Uffizi) for the Tuscan State. The most outstanding thing about the design of the Uffizi is the way in which the long tunnel-like shape is accepted and used for its dramatic effect. The actual details of the work are rather unimaginative, with one or two exceptions which are by Buontalenti after Vasari's death.

[158]

157 Palazzo Pitti, the Garden front,
by Amannati, begun *c.* 1558

158 The Uffizi, from the Arno Loggia, by
Vasari, from 1560

159 The Uffizi, Porta delle Suppliche, by
Buontalenti, after 1574

Bernardo Buontalenti was born about 1536 and died in 1608. He was the major architect of the last years of the sixteenth century in Florence but he was also active as a painter, sculptor, and fireworks expert and his whole career was spent in the service of the Medici. For them he built the splendid Villa Pratolino near Florence, now destroyed, and in 1574 he succeeded Vasari at the Uffizi, where he designed the extraordinary Porta delle Suppliche, with its pediment broken into two pieces set back to back, a fantasy which even Michelangelo had not attempted. In the same year he designed an equally bizarre flight of steps for the altar of SS. Trinita (now in Sto Stefano) and also began the Casino Mediceo near S. Marco. In 1593–4 he built the new façade of SS. Trinita, and his last work was the Loggia de' Banchi in Pisa, begun in 1605. The influence of Michelangelo was thus continued until at least the end of the century.

[159]

Perhaps the finest architect of the later sixteenth century was Andrea Palladio, who was born in 1508 and died in 1580. Almost all his life was spent in the small city of Vicenza and almost all his works are in the city or the surrounding countryside. He was to become one of the great formative influences on English architecture and his influence was exercised partly through his publications, of which the most important was his treatise *I Quattro Libri dell'Architettura*. This was first published in 1570 and contains illustrations of the classical orders, a series of selected antique buildings, and illustrations of most of Palladio's own works. It is far more learned and precise than Serlio's treatise and has a much greater range than Vignola's. Inigo Jones studied it deeply and through him Palladio's ideas came to be the mainspring of English eighteenth-century architecture. There is a large collection of Palladio's drawings in the Royal Institute of British Architects and these, together with the treatise, give us a very good idea of the basis of his style, which is essentially classical and Bramantesque, although influenced – like that of every other artist in the sixteenth century – by the works of Michelangelo. The classical elements in his style derive from a close study at first hand of the monuments in Rome, which he visited on several occasions. Although he was the son of a miller he soon came under the notice of the humanist Trissino, who gave him a classical education, took him to Rome, and bestowed on him the name Palladio, derived from Pallas. The Roman monuments were drawn by him in great

[160, 161]

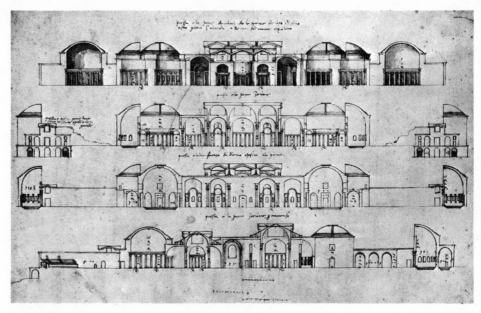

160 Palladio's reconstruction of the Baths of Titus, Rome

161 Vicenza, Palazzo Porto-Colleoni. Drawing by Palladio

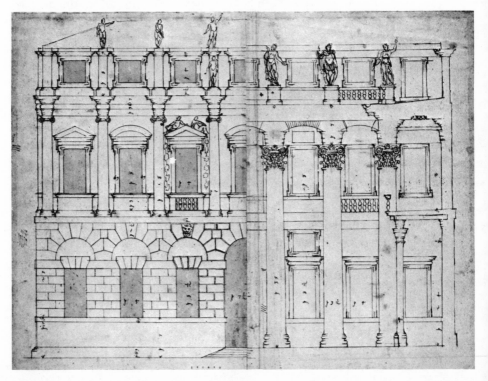

162 Vicenza, Basilica Palladiana. Palladio, 1549 and later

[160] detail and reconstructed with rather more sense of grandeur than of
actuality, but it is clear from the tendency of his mind that Bramante
and Vignola would be the modern architects who appealed most
strongly to him. Such Mannerist elements as there are in Palladio's
work seem to derive from Michelangelo's buildings of the 1540s
and later; but it is likely also that he was predisposed in this direction
by the study of some of the richer monuments of classical antiquity.
Palladio also provided a series of illustrations for the best of the
[163] numerous sixteenth-century editions of Vitruvius, that by Bishop
Barbaro of 1556.

[162] The first building which made his name was the recasing of the
old Basilica, or Town Hall, in Vicenza itself. Palladio's model was
accepted by the Town Council in 1549, when they rejected the
model submitted by Giulio Romano (who had died in 1546). It is
evident that Palladio's praise of Sansovino's Library in Venice was
sincere; for his solution to the problem of supporting the old Basilica
was to buttress it externally by a double loggia very similar in type
to the forms used by Sansovino and similar also to a drawing published in Serlio's treatise. The elements used in the construction of the

212

Basilica are very simple. Since it was a basilica (and therefore connected in Palladio's mind with the classical idea of a grand public building) his basic solution was necessarily conditioned by the use of the orders; Doric on the ground floor and Ionic on the upper. The great piers with attached columns provide the support and the spaces between these points of support can then be filled with the large arches and smaller columns which are parts of the so-called Palladian motive. The architectural effect is thus dependent on the play of light and shade in the arches themselves, opposed to the solid masses of masonry; but it is due also to the great subtlety of the actual shapes of the openings and the architectural elements. Unlike Sansovino, Palladio breaks the entablature forward over each of his columns, emphasizing the projections rather than the horizontal quality which is so marked a feature of the Library. The proportions of the arched openings, the smaller rectangular side spaces, and the circular openings above them have all been most carefully considered, and there is a final touch in the way in which the motives at the angles have narrower side openings so that the effect of the doubled columns at each end is greatly increased and the angles of the building appear solid and heavy.

The evolution of Palladio's style can be seen in the palaces which he built in Vicenza itself, and a few of them, of different dates, will show the general trend of his ideas. One of the earliest, the Palazzo Porto of 1552, is clearly derived from Bramante's House of Raphael [161, 165]

163 Palladio's reconstruction of a Roman Theatre from Barbaro's *Vitruvius*, 1556

design with the addition of some rather Michelangelesque sculpture over the windows of the centre and end bays. The general effect is [166] therefore very similar indeed to Sanmicheli's palaces in Verona. The plan, however, reveals a different aspect of Palladio since it shows a reconstruction of the ancient type of house with symmetrically disposed blocks on either side of a great square courtyard with a Giant Order of columns all round it, obviously intended as a reconstruction of the classical atrium. Another point about the plan is of even greater importance, since it shows the passion for absolute symmetry and also the sequence of room shapes, each proportioned to the one next to it, which were to become the basic principles of Palladio's villas. Thus the rooms at the left of the plan begin with the central hall 30 feet square leading into a room 30 by 20 feet which in turn leads into one 20 feet square. This combination of classical forms, mathematical harmonies, and symmetrical disposition is what makes Palladio's architecture perennially fascinating and what caused the architects of the eighteenth century to imitate him so closely. Much of this is, of course, founded on the study of Vitruvius as well as on actual Roman buildings, and it is evident that the atrium in the Palazzo Porto, or the description of the Basilica given by Vitruvius, were much in his mind in the 1550s when he was preparing the illustrations for Barbaro's edition. A similar classical reminiscence is [164] to be found in the odd, but very beautiful, Palazzo Chiericati which was begun in the 1550s as part of a projected forum, so that the

164 Palazzo Chiericati, begun 1550s

present open colonnades were intended to be part of a town-planning design rather than part of a single building as they now are. The palace, which is now the Museum of Vicenza, is relatively small and the great, open loggie take up a disproportionate amount of space, but they are nevertheless superb examples of the Doric and Ionic orders treated in a more austerely classical manner than the superimposed arches of Sansovino's Library in Venice. The Palazzo Thiene of a few years later reflects current Mannerist interests in [*167, 168*] textures as well as a new interest in the shapes of rooms. The plan shows that all the rooms are still proportioned one to another, but they now have the added interest of great variety of shape. This feature derives from Roman Baths and was part of Palladio's adaptation of classical themes to modern domestic use. The drawing used for the *Quattro Libri* differs slightly from the executed façade and shows some influence from Giulio Romano in the heavily rusticated masonry and especially in the rough keystones above the windows. The unusual idea of a series of swags level with the capitals – which was omitted in the executed building – was copied by Inigo Jones in the Banqueting House in Whitehall, which owes a great deal to the Palazzo Thiene. Ten years later, in 1566, came the Palazzo Valmarana. [*170*] The drawing in the R.I.B.A. collection shows two of the most curious features of this palace. One is the extremely Mannerist treatment of the end bay with a pedimented window and a statue, where all the other bays of the *piano nobile* have rectangular windows

165, 166 Palazzo Porto, 1552. Façade, section and plan

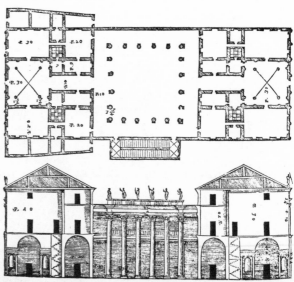

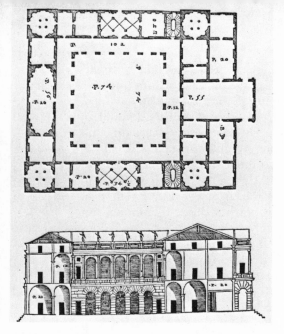

167, 168 Palazzo Thiene, 1550s(?). Plan, section and façade

set between the columns of a Giant Order. The use of a Giant Order with smaller pilasters on the ground floor supporting a straight entablature is certainly derived from Michelangelo's palaces on the Capitol, but some of the other features, notably the texture of the rustication, can be traced back to classical prototypes rather than to contemporary Mannerism. In his late palaces Palladio adopted Michelangelo's Giant Order as well as some of the Mannerist elements

[169] of richness in decoration. The fragment of the palace known as the 'Casa del Diavolo', but actually another palace for the Porto family, of 1571, shows this clearly and attractively.

In the last months of his life Palladio designed and began a theatre for an Academy in Vicenza of which he himself was a member. This, as one might expect, is a thorough-going attempt to reconstruct

[163] the antique Roman theatre as described by Vitruvius, and as known from one or two surviving examples.

[171–73] The Teatro Olimpico is based on the ancient Roman principle of a fixed and elaborate architectural backdrop or proscenium with the stage in front of it. The auditorium is semicircular, or in this case half-elliptical, with tiers of seats rising sharply to the level of a

216

169 Palazzo Porto-Breganza ('Casa del Diavolo'), 1571

170 Palazzo Valmarana, 1566

colonnade which runs round the back of the theatre. In the classical examples the auditorium was open to the sky, but Palladio's small theatre is roofed over and has sky and clouds painted on the flat ceiling. The most fascinating part of the whole elaborate structure is the permanent stage setting behind the proscenium. This was executed by Palladio's pupil Scamozzi, but undoubtedly follows Palladio's own ideas. The section together with the plan shows that an elaborate perspective effect is obtained in a very small space by sloping the backstage part upwards and narrowing the passageways to give an accelerated perspective effect to the streets. It is possible also to obtain effects of lighting by stationing men with torches inside the scenery.

A similar effect can be seen in two of the very few churches which he built. In Venice the church of S. Francesco della Vigna has a façade by Palladio, and the churches of S. Giorgio Maggiore and the Redentore are both entirely by him. All are late works, S. Giorgio having been begun in 1566 and the Redentore ten years later, as a votive offering for the cessation of a particularly bad outbreak of plague. Both these churches represent Palladio at the height of his powers, and both have marked peculiarities in plan which, at first

[174–81]

217

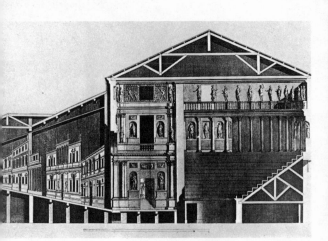
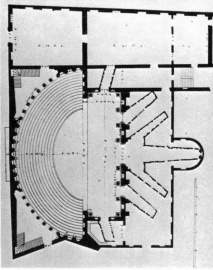

171 Section, showing perspective scenery (stage on left)   172 Plan (stage on right)

sight, seem far removed from the strictly symmetrical planning so characteristic of Palladio's villas.

The façades of both churches, and also that of the earlier S. Francesco della Vigna, present new solutions to the old problem of designing a completely classical façade for a basilican type of building which, although it existed in antiquity, was known to sixteenth-century architects only from the reconstructions made by the editors of Vitruvius such as, for example, Barbaro and Palladio. The problem arose from the fact that the ancient temple was a building with a single, gabled, end which could easily be expressed in terms of free-standing columns supporting a pediment. The earliest Christian churches, however, were based on the ancient basilica, which was a secular building, rather than on pagan temples. The basilica had a high central nave, with one or more low aisles on each side, and the architectural treatment of such a front presented considerable problems which Early Christian architects tended either to ignore or to evade by the provision of some kind of loggia or atrium masking the junction of aisles and nave. Thus, churches like Old St Peter's, or the Lateran before its rebuilding in the seventeenth century, presented a main entrance which lacked the dignity of the classical temple front. The first steps towards a solution to the problem of

VICENZA,
THE TEATRO OLIMPICO
by Palladio, 1580;
completed by Scamozzi

173 Interior showing perspectives

combining the antique temple with the Christian church façade had been taken in the 1460s and 1470s by Alberti.

In all three of his Venetian church façades Palladio evolved a solution based on the idea of interlocking two separate temple fronts. At S. Francesco and S. Giorgio Maggiore the nave is treated as a [176] high but narrow temple, with four large columns on high bases supporting a strongly marked pediment. Behind these columns there appears to run a continuous cornice which forms the lower part of a second, much wider, pediment supported on numerous small columns and extending the full width of the church. The same idea carried a stage further can be seen in the Redentore which has three [180] pediments, the large central one being set against a high, rectangular, attic. The total effect is very compact and builds up the composition towards the great dome. In this case, however, the side parts of the church are not true aisles but, as the plan shows, merely the end walls of the side chapels. The plan of the entrance façade is, therefore, similar to the almost contemporary Gesù in Rome, although the [148] Redentore façade is considerably closer to antique prototypes.

Even more than in the complexities of the façades, the eastern parts of the plans of S. Giorgio and the Redentore differ from contemporary churches such as the Gesù; and they seem to have almost no

219

connection with earlier churches or, indeed, with the ideas on church design expressed by Palladio himself in his book. Palladio's statement that he made the church of S. Giorgio Maggiore in the shape of a cross for symbolic reasons is not very convincing, since almost any traditional Latin cross church plan would be far more obviously symbolic than this shortened and widened cross form, with apses terminating the choir and transepts. The similarity between S. Giorgio and the Redentore can, in fact, be explained only in terms of their function, since both churches were visited in state by the Doge once a year. It was a Venetian custom, which lasted down to the end of the Republic, that the Doge should make ten solemn *Andate* each year to various churches, in connection with events associated with them.

Since the early thirteenth century the Benedictine monastery on the island of S. Giorgio had possessed what was said to be the body of St Stephen. On St Stephen's Day, 26 December, the Doge made a solemn procession from St Mark's across the Grand Canal to S. Giorgio bringing with him the choir of St Mark's and a large crowd of spectators. In combination with the Benedictine community a solemn Mass was celebrated, sung by the two choirs. Since S. Giorgio was a Benedictine house, which also served as an official residence for distinguished visitors to the Republic, the church had, from the beginning, to contain a monks' choir in which the daily obligation of singing the Divine Office could be performed by day and by night. At the same time, the church had to be large enough

VENICE, S, GIORGIO MAGGIORE by Palladio, begun 1566

174 Plan   175 Section

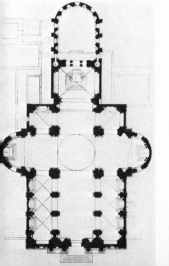

to contain the vast crowd which accompanied the Doge on his annual visit.

In the case of the Redentore there was no established procession because the church itself, as we learn from the dedicatory inscription – CHRISTO REDEMPTORI CIVITATE GRAVI PESTILENTIA LIBERATA SENATUS EX VOTO PRID. NON. SEPT. AN. MDLXXVI. – was built as a State commission, following the cessation of the great plague of 1576. When the Senate resolution was taken to build the church it was decided that the Doge should make an *andata* on the third Sunday in July, as an act of thanksgiving, and we know that in this case the ceremony, although not quite so elaborate as that at S. Giorgio, also involved the participation of the Franciscans who served the church, and the Doge's choir from St Mark's. Both churches, therefore, have in common the fact that on one day in the year they had to house much larger congregations than normal, and an imported choir had to be accommodated as well as the monastic choirs.

One other factor determines the design of these two churches, so similar to each other and so unlike any others: during the sixteenth century the choir of St Mark's was undoubtedly one of the finest in the world, and under its choir-masters Adriaen Willaerts and Andrea and Giovanni Gabrieli, it had developed a technique of exploiting the resonance of St Mark's by splitting up into separate choirs, widely spaced in the building. From this there grew a tradition of writing for several choirs singing separately or together, and the design of these

176 Façade   177 Interior

two churches is therefore the most practical solution for the problems set, bearing in mind that the choir of St Mark's was accustomed to sing in at least two separate parts.

There is a letter written by Palladio to a friend in Vicenza which gives a good idea of the genesis of the Redentore. To begin with, there was some debate over the shape to be taken by the new church and at least fifty members of the Senate were in favour of a centrally planned building. Twice as many, however, were in favour of a Latin cross plan and it was decided to ask Palladio to submit models of each type, the Latin cross one being officially chosen. In all probability, Palladio himself would have preferred a circular or square plan since he had written, as recently as 1570: 'In order to observe Decorum in the form of temples [we] will choose the most perfect and excellent, which is the circle; for it alone is simple, uniform, equal, strong, and adapted to its purpose . . . most apt to demonstrate the Unity, the infinite Essence, the Uniformity and Justice of God.' Nevertheless, it is probable that Palladio realized well enough that the only feasible solution to the problem set was the shape which he had himself invented ten years earlier for S. Giorgio. Certainly, the Latin cross type would have been more generally acceptable, and Palladio must have seemed rather old fashioned in the way in which he maintained the ideals of the generation of Bramante.

From the point of view of architectural form, perhaps the most striking feature about both churches is the invention of the open screen through which the spectator in the nave gets a glimpse of the monastic

VENICE, IL REDENTORE by Palladio, 1576

178 Plan   179 Section

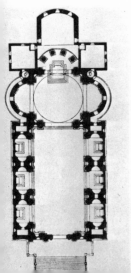
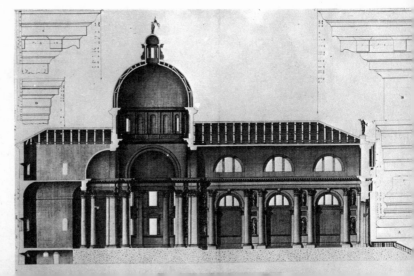

choir. In S. Giorgio this is a comparatively simple effect with a straight wall opened up and supported on two columns immediately behind the High Altar. The effect of the sound of the monks' choir filtering through the colonnade is extraordinarily impressive, but the architectural form is still simple and can be paralleled in ancient architecture (cf. plate 160), although, of course, it was not used there to produce acoustic effects.

The Redentore is a more complex version of the same theme since the semicircular form of the colonnade, striking in itself, makes it seem that the spectator is looking through the apse of the church. The effect of alternate open and closed spaces is greatly heightened by the [181] projecting columns which close the end of the nave so that, standing there, the spectator is in a rectangular space bounded at the east by a flight of steps and the strongly projecting walls and columns, beyond which the crossing is perceived as a closed, circular, space rising up into the dome and reopened at the east end by the screen of columns. The play of light changes constantly in the simple, pale, interior, so that there is an almost endless succession of spatial effects, varying according to the time of day and the season of the year.

Most of Palladio's ideas, and especially his principles of harmonic proportion, can be seen in the very numerous villas he built in and around Vicenza, many of which still survive, while others are known to us from plates in his book. These villas, however, are best considered in relationship to other villas of the sixteenth century, such as those by Vignola, and may be taken together in a separate chapter.

180 Façade

181 Interior

Villas: Vignola and Palladio

Town life, as we know it, began early in Italy; and for this very reason the somewhat sentimental nostalgia for the joys of country life which is so marked a feature of modern urban living began in Italy in the late fourteenth or early fifteenth century. It was given expression by Villani in 1338 and slightly later by Boccaccio and Petrarch; but it is more than likely that all these writers were not so much filled with enthusiasm for the country as producing deliberate imitations of a classical literary form. This peculiar affliction of the town-dweller was certainly known to the ancient Romans and the desire to escape to a country retreat which should be both peaceful and civilized appears in the letters of Pliny the Younger. The Villa Madama was an attempt to reconstruct a classical Roman *villa suburbana* as described by Pliny, and for the next two centuries such villas multiplied in the countryside around Rome, particularly at Frascati and Tivoli. As early as the mid fifteenth century Alberti, in his treatise, drew the distinction which the ancients had made between the villa proper, which is a working farm, and the *villa suburbana*, which was always just outside the walls of a town and was intended purely for pleasure and for a very short stay. Most of the suburban villas, such as the Palazzo del Tè, were so close to the town that they contained no bedrooms and were intended solely as a place in which to pass a very hot day in peace and quiet. Many such villas were built outside Florence and a few still survive, but naturally there has been much destruction and many were destroyed during the Siege of 1529. These villas, and the even more important ones in the Veneto, belonged to wealthy families and were often self-supporting in the sense that the farm attached to the villa provided the town-house with corn, oil, and wine; but an entirely different type of villa is represented by the buildings of the cardinals and some of the popes, following the lead of Gregory XIII (1572–85), who began to build in the hills outside Rome.

The majority of these villas, many of which still survive, were built by the cardinal members of the great Italian families who still own them. These differ from the type common in the north in that they were much more elaborate and often have very beautiful gardens, while the northern type almost always remained essentially a farm. Two of the most superb of the former type of villa were built by Vignola, one for Pope Julius III, the Villa Giulia, now the Museum of Etruscan Antiquities, on the edge of Rome itself; while the other, which is now the official summer residence of the President of Italy, was the huge castle at Caprarola near Viterbo. The Villa Giulia was Vignola's first major commission but it is not quite certain how much of it is his; the building was put up between 1550 and 1555 and we know that both Vignola and Amannati were employed on it, with Vasari as a sort of overseer, and with both Michelangelo and the Pope himself taking a hand in the design. Nevertheless, it seems certain that the house is by Vignola and the garden part with its buildings by Amannati. A medal of 1553 shows that the building as executed is essentially in accordance with the original design, although two small domes have been omitted. The plan shows that Julius III undoubtedly intended an allusion to the Belvedere built by his predecessor Julius II, while a half-circular court at the back of the building equally clearly recalls the Villa Madama and, like it, is intended to refer to Pliny's descriptions. The marked contrast between the outside and the inside of the villa on plan is retained in the elevation. The front of the build-ing is simple, and rather austere, with a certain amount of texture in the window surrounds and with a marked emphasis on the vertical, central, element like a double triumphal arch. The main entrance, which is also a triumphal arch in form, has heavy rustication of the type associated both with Vignola and with Amannati and this, together with the formality of the triumphal arch motifs, provides a severe entrance front. The villa itself, or Casino, is very small since the building was not intended to be lived in and is quite a short distance from the Vatican Palace. Once one has passed through the main entrance the rear façade provides a striking contrast, since it consists of a semicircular colonnade with smooth panelled surfaces above it. The link between it and the exterior façade is provided by the repetition of the triumphal arch motive in the centre and the large arches at either end. The colonnade proper has straight entablatures over the columns, a form almost certainly borrowed by Vignola from Michelangelo's Capitoline Palaces.

The curved shape and the finely cut modelling of the villa contrast with the loggia, or Nymphaeum, which marks the centre of the

[182–85]

[184]

[185]

[182]

[183]

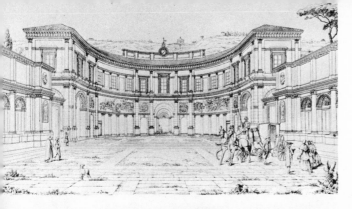

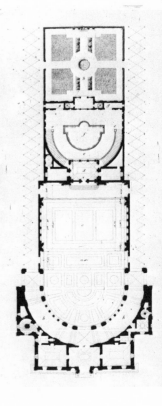

ROME, VILLA GIULIA
by Vignola, Amannati
and others, 1550–55

182 Garden front

183 Nymphaeum

184 Plan

185 Façade

garden. This, which is by Amannatı, repeats the disposition of the villa in that it has a straight façade with a deep re-entrant curve at the back, which in this case consists of two flights of steps leading downwards into the water garden. As one might imagine, the architectural forms employed in the garden parts are freer and more fanciful than those of the house itself and it is a tribute both to Julius III and to his advisers that Vignola and Amannati worked together so successfully on what was the first major commission for each of them.

The villa at Caprarola is rather different, since it was begun in the [*186–88*] early 1520s by Antonio da Sangallo the Younger and Peruzzi. It was the headquarters of the newly-rich Farnese family and stood in the centre of their vast possessions. Probably for this reason the great building has the curious shape of a pentagon, since at that moment the pentagon was a favourite type of fortress plan. This shape, together with the completely circular inner courtyard, was fixed by the earlier architects; Vignola took over in 1559 and continued to work on the building until his death in 1573. The frontal view shows the great bastions and the pentagonal shape established by the first architects, who probably also planned the loggia at the bottom and the great flights of steps. The front door is illustrated in Vignola's treatise and is therefore presumably by him, while the style of the upper part of the building from the *piano nobile* upwards is unmistakably his. The division into vertical elements with plain surfaces at the ends and a decorative texture obtained by quoins at the angles is a characteristic of his style; and so is the flat, panel-like effect of the pilasters and the mouldings of the loggia on the first floor. At either end of the open loggia there is a closed bay with a window head very similar to those in the Villa Giulia. The upper part of the building consists of a storey with an attic above it linked by pilasters arranged above those on the *piano nobile*. The façade shows the cramped and uncomfortable disposition of the rooms, and these upper storeys are awkwardly contrived to fit in behind the pilasters. The problem here was to find sufficient accommodation for the large number of retainers who accompanied the family on their visits, while at the same time providing quarters for the permanent residents. The villa at Caprarola is thus not a villa in the strict sense of the word but is often, more correctly, referred to as a castle. The internal court is once more based on Pliny's description of a circular court, but is made up of elements very reminiscent of Bramante. The rusticated ground floor with pairs

CAPRAROLA,
VILLA FARNESE
by Vignola, from 1559

186 General view

187 Court

188 Diagram showing plan
and section

[81]

of columns alternating with openings on the upper floor is a restatement of Bramante's House of Raphael, while the bays themselves – a
small rectangular opening flanked by half-columns followed by a
large round-headed opening – are almost exactly the same as
Bramante's basic form in the Belvedere. A significant detail linking
the two buildings is the way in which the cornice breaks forward
over both columns while the bases are separate. Finally, the superb
and richly decorated spiral staircase is an enlarged version of the
famous example by Bramante in the Belvedere.

228

189 Careggi,
altered by Michelozzo

190 Poggio a Caiano,
by Giuliano da Sangallo,
1480s

The simpler type of farmhouse villa can be traced back to Florentine examples, some of which belonged to the Medici family. Two of the most important Medicean villas are those at Careggi and Poggio a   [*189, 190*] Caiano. Careggi was originally a fourteenth-century farmhouse, but was altered by Michelozzo in the fifteenth century. The later and grander villa at Poggio a Caiano was transformed in the 1480s by Giuliano da Sangallo. The present horseshoe-shaped staircase dates from the seventeenth century, but the wide, rather ill-proportioned colonnade with a pediment above it is probably the earliest application

229

of a classical temple front to a villa. The plan of Poggio a Caiano is also strictly symmetrical, and these are the two characteristics which are the essential features of all the numerous villas by Palladio. Palladio was not the first to build villas in Venetian territory, since there were at least two important prototypes by Sansovino and Sanmicheli. The Villa La Soranza by Sanmicheli was built about 1545–55 but has now been destroyed. The Villa Garzone by Sansovino is of about 1540 and is particularly important, since it consists of a double loggia with projecting wings, all arranged according to symmetry and stated in terms of High Renaissance architecture. Sanmicheli's lost villa is known to have used linking walls to connect the main block of buildings with the farm buildings and this was also an idea taken up and developed by Palladio. Nevertheless, the most important single influence on the Palladian type of villa was provided by Trissino, who

[191]

191 Pontecasale, Villa Garzone, by Sansovino, c. 1540

192, 193 Cricoli, near Vicenza, Villa Trissino, by Trissino, 1536/7

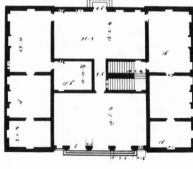

trained Palladio, and who built himself a villa about 1536/7 which precedes both the Villa Garzone and the Villa La Soranza. This, the Villa Cricoli, was based on the descriptions in Vitruvius and the plate in Serlio's book of the Villa Madama; but on the whole it seems closest to the Farnesina in Rome, which Trissino must have known. The Villa Cricoli consists of a double loggia, framed by flanking towers which project very slightly so that the basic form of the plan is similar to the Farnesina, except in the projection of the wings. The plan shows the rigid symmetry of the disposition and it also shows the other major characteristic of Palladio's villas, namely the arrangement of the rooms in such a way that each room is not only mathematically proportioned in itself but is part of a sequence with its neighbours to form a total mathematical harmony. Thus each of the three rooms in the side parts is the same width, but the lengths vary so that the centre

[*192, 193*]

[*193, 111*]

194, 195 Lonedo, Villa Godi, by Palladio, *c.* 1538

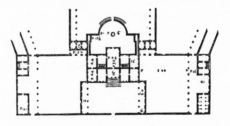

room is square while the side rooms are roughly 3:2 in their proportions in each case. In practice Palladio quite frequently departed from this principle, but the illustrations given in his treatise, with the figures inscribed on the plans, make it clear that he attached the greatest importance to the principle itself.

[194, 195]   Palladio's own first attempt, the Villa Godi at Lonedo, is somewhat less effective, particularly in the façade, than was Trissino's. The plan and elevation given in the *Quattro Libri* of 1570 have obviously been tidied up and represent Palladio's mature ideas on villa planning. The principle of linking farm buildings with the house is represented in the plan by walls and colonnades, while the principle of the varied sequence of the rooms can be seen from the figures 16:24:36 which condition the sizes of the rooms. The central element, with a flight of steps leading up to the triple-arched entrance, is recessed but it projects by an equal amount at the back of the design so that the shape as a whole, as in all Palladio's villas, is roughly cubical. Only one feature is lacking in this design which is to be found in his more mature works. This is the application of a classical temple front
[196, 197]   to a country-house, and even here it might be argued that the triple-arched entrance represents the idea in a crude form. It can be seen in all his developed plans such as, for example, the Villa Malcontenta of 1560.

Palladio had an immense knowledge of antique architecture, but he could hardly have known anything about ancient villas at first hand, and the descriptions in Vitruvius and Pliny are notoriously vague. His knowledge of temples and public buildings led him to believe, quite erroneously, that the ancients 'very probably took the idea and the reason from private buildings; that is, from houses', and he therefore designed all his villas with an impressive entrance portico. This, in the strong sunshine of Italy, has much to recommend it, but it should be remembered that many English and American country-houses have enormous, inconvenient, and draughty porticoes simply because Palladio misinterpreted ancient architecture: yet the spell of his own works was so strong on all English architects of the eighteenth century that they copied this feature irrespective of its impracticability in a northern climate.

The Villa Malcontenta is traditionally said to derive its name from a discontented woman who lived there, but it seems difficult to believe that anyone could live by the side of the Brenta Canal in such a beautiful house and remain discontented, though its former rather

196 Villa Malcontenta,
near Mestre, 1560

197 Villa Rotonda, Vicenza,
begun *c.* 1567/9

198 Villa Malcontenta,
plan and section

199 Villa Rotonda, Vicenza,
plan and section

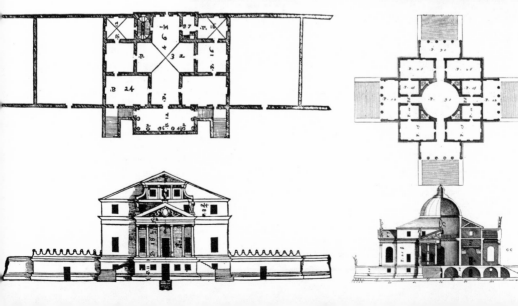

[197, 199]

ruinous condition might well have induced a pleasing melancholy. The portico is the principal feature of the house, standing on a high base with a flight of steps on either side. The plan shows a typical arrangement of rooms based on a block which is half as wide again as it is deep, with a great central cruciform hall with the rooms arranged round the arms of the cross in a carefully calculated rhythmical proportion. Most of Palladio's villas have the principal room in the centre and many of them have this room lit by a dome. This can be seen in the most rigidly symmetrical of all, the Villa Rotonda just outside Vicenza, which was begun about 1567/9. This is, properly speaking, a *villa suburbana* and was therefore, in Palladio's mind, a rather more formal building. The plan shows that the house is completely symmetrical round the circular central hall, and the symmetry is carried so far that the main entrance portico is actually repeated on the other three sides. The formal beauty of the Villa Rotonda has always caused it to hold a high place among Palladio's works and there were at one time at least three copies of it built in England, one of which, Lord Burlington's villa at Chiswick, is one of the masterpieces of English architecture and in some ways an improvement on its model. The Villa Rotonda was completed after Palladio's death by his pupil Vincenzo Scamozzi, who was born in 1552 and died in 1616. Scamozzi altered the shape of the dome and raised the attic, as may be seen by comparing the photograph with the woodcut in Palladio's book. Scamozzi is best known as the designer of the Procuratie Nuove, which is the principal feature of St Mark's Square in Venice, matching Sansovino's Library. He also wrote a very large treatise[33] on

200 Project for a Villa for the Mocenigo family, never executed. From Palladio's *I Quattro Libri . . .*, 1570

201 Palladio's villa at Maser, *c.* 1560, with frescoes by Veronese

architecture and designed a number of villas in the Palladian style;
the best known of these is the Villa Molin, near Padua, of about 1597.
This was one of the principal influences on Inigo Jones when he
designed the Queen's House at Greenwich, although Jones met
Scamozzi himself in Venice and was not at all impressed by him.
They apparently disagreed on some architectural questions and Jones
noted crossly 'but this Scamozzi, being purblind, could not see'.

Another of Palladio's late villas which was very influential on
English architecture, although the building was never executed, was
the design made for Leonardo Mocenigo for a villa on the Brenta,   [200]
which he reproduced as the last of his designs for villas. This is
particularly interesting and complex since it consists of a large
cubical block with a portico on each front, and with an atrium at the
centre of the house. The dependent buildings are linked to the main
block by four symmetrically disposed quadrant colonnades, so that
there are two main views: one, from the side, with the portico set
between two rectangular blocks, and the more important view from
back and front in which, in Palladio's own words, the colonnades
reach forward like arms, as if to greet the visitor.

The Villa Maser is also of about 1560 and is a well-preserved example
of the simple farm type; but the great glory of this villa is not so much

[201] Palladio's architecture as the wonderful series of illusionistic frescoes by Veronese. This is one of the earliest modern examples of landscape painting on a large scale for its own sake, although such frescoes were certainly painted in ancient villas, and the combination of great architecture and great painting is one of the happiest moments of the Italian Renaissance. It was precisely this ability to combine two or more of the arts which was to be one of the features of the Baroque style, and it can be seen also in the palatial villas at Tivoli and Frascati. The Villa D'Este, of the middle of the sixteenth century, is famous for its wonderful gardens with scores of fountains and rows of cypress trees. The Villa Mondragone, of the 1570s, is also a superb example of the siting of a comparatively simple building so as to obtain the maximum effect from the fall of the land and the combination of

[202] natural and architectural beauty. It is perhaps appropriate to end this book with the Villa Aldobrandini built by Giacomo della Porta between 1598 and 1603. The villa itself with its huge broken pediment is a good example of della Porta's Mannerist style; but its greatest beauty lies in the combination of rich decorative sculpture, simple architectural forms, natural verdure, and those wonderful fountains whose music echoes through the Roman night.

202 Frascati, Villa Aldobrandini. Giacomo della Porta, 1598–1603

Notes to text

1 This version, one of at least two, is quoted from the translation given in E. G. Holt, *A Documentary History of Art*, New York, 1957, I, 291 ff.

2 Quoted from *The Renaissance Reader*, ed. J. B. Ross and M. M. McLaughlin, New York, 1958, 384.

3 The idea of the perfection of the circle as a reflection of God's perfection was not invented by Palladio – it can be found, more than a century earlier, in the writings of Cardinal Nicholas of Cusa: 'In Him . . . the beginning is such that the end and the beginning are one. . . . All this we gather from the infinite circle, which, having neither beginning nor end, is eternal, infinitely one and infinite in capacity.' Cf. P. Burke, *The Renaissance*, London, 1964, 73–4.

4 E. Mâle, *The Early Churches of Rome*, London, 1960, 29.

5 An axonometric drawing consists of a plan which is set up truly but turned to a convenient angle. The verticals are then drawn on this and to scale. By these means, all the horizontal and all the vertical elements of the building are represented correctly and to the same scale. Anything which is neither truly vertical nor horizontal becomes distorted; but an axonometric drawing, once one has learnt to disregard the distortions, can teach a very great deal about structure.

6 The vaulting of the Temple of 'Minerva Medica' in Rome, which was still covered in Brunelleschi's day, may well have given him the idea even though it is not, strictly speaking, carried on pendentives.

7 Cf. *Architectural Principles*, 3rd ed., 1962, 47 ff.

8 Sta Croce, however, survives only in mutilated form.

9 In 1310 the Arte dei Medici e Speziali covered one hundred occupations.

10 Cf. *Memoirs of a Renaissance Pope*, ed. F. A. Gragg and L. C. Gabel, New York, 1959, 282–91.

11 *Ibid.*, 289.

12 'Federicus, Montis Feretri Urbini etc. . . . We have searched everywhere, and especially in Tuscany (which is the fountainhead of architects) without finding a really skilled man, learned in the said mystery; but at last we learned of the reputation – which has been confirmed by experience – of the excellent Master Lutiano, bearer of this patent. . . . We have appointed the said Master Lutiano as Overseer and the Head of all the masters working [on the Palace] . . . 10 June 1468.'

13 Perhaps something like the top storey of the Palazzo della Cancelleria?

14 Federigo was made Duke in 1474. Those inscriptions which refer to 'CO[MES] [Count]' must be earlier than 1474; those which refer to 'DVX' must be of 1474 or later. Federigo died in 1482.

15 Leonardo's projected treatise on anatomy contains the following passage: 'You will become acquainted with every part . . . by means of a demonstration from three different aspects; for, when you have seen a member from the front . . . you will be shown the same member from the side or from behind, just as if you had the

actual member in your hand and went on turning it from side to side until you had a full understanding. . . .'

16 Cf. Sangallo's Sacristy at Sto Spirito (plate 25).

17 E.g. The Church of the Nativity, at Bethlehem, and the Holy Sepulchre, Jerusalem.

18 It has been altered: cf. plates 75 and 76.

19 The engraving (plate 78) shows the ideal; in fact, the servants had to sleep somewhere, and the drawing (plate 79) shows attic windows between the metopes. Later palaces show how this problem was often solved in a similar way – cf. plate 103.

20 Traditionally this palace was begun in 1515, but there have recently been attempts to date it later, and, therefore, to deny the attribution to Raphael. Vasari attributed it to Lorenzetto, Raphael's assistant.

21 The alternative date 1492 (implied by Vasari) seems inherently more probable, although the document which records Giulio's death in hospital in Mantua on 1 November 1546, at the age of forty-seven, would seem to make 1499 almost certain: nevertheless, Vasari got much of his information from Giulio himself, and the earlier date makes the evolution of Giulio's style much more comprehensible.

22 The Romans defined villas as *suburbana* and *rustica*. The suburban type was near enough to the city to need no bedrooms, since it was not intended for residence. The *villa rustica*, on the other hand, was more an independent country-house with farms.

23 It was probably Roman in origin, was first used in the Renaissance by Bramante, and is known in Italian as a *serliana*, after Serlio.

24 The palace is the French Embassy in Rome, but is open to the public on Sunday mornings.

25 It is difficult to be dogmatic about this, since there are many earlier buildings which have a large order uniting a ground floor and a mezzanine storey so big that it might almost count as a second storey.

26 A document has recently been published which shows, however, that the chapel was in progress as early as 1529.

27 This explains why references to 1570 can be found in modern editions of a book apparently published in 1568. Both versions are conveniently available in the Club del Libro edition, Milan, vol. VII, 1965.

28 In the Doric order (as on the ground floor of the Library in Figure 138) the frieze above the columns consists of an alternation of square fields sometimes carved with sculpture in relief (metopes) and three vertical bars with channelling (triglyphs).

29 It was first published in 1966, in Milan.

30 In 1968 it was still in a deplorable state.

31 Ultimately, all these derive from the form invented by Alberti at Sta Maria Novella, Florence, about 1450, and introduced into Rome in the fifteenth century at S. Agostino and Sta Maria del Popolo.

32 The Lateran is a weak derivative from the Palazzo Farnese.

33 *Dell' Idea dell' Architettura universale*, Venice, 1615. First translated into English in 1669.

Bibliographical note

This list of books for further reading is divided into two quite separate parts. In the first there are notes on the earliest treatises and source-books, treated in some detail. Since this book first appeared, twenty years ago, there has been considerable activity in reprinting facsimile editions of architectural classics and, as far as possible, these reprints have been noted for this new edition. The second part consists of a list of books, mostly of recent date, which deal with the period in general. This is followed by monographs and some books on individual buildings or problems, as far as possible in English; there are, of course, many very important works in Italian or German but these, like periodical literature, can be found in the bibliographies in most of the books cited here.

1 The sources

The impetus to treatise-writing came from the descriptions given by Pliny the Younger in his *Letters*, of which many editions appeared in the fifteenth century; and, even more, from the only surviving ancient technical treatise, *De architectura libri X.* by Vitruvius, several MSS of which were known in Italy in the fifteenth century. The first printed edition – the *editio princeps* – was issued at Rome, probably in 1486; several other editions followed rapidly but the first good Latin text, with a commentary and illustrations, is that by Fra Giocondo, Venice, 1511 (and 1513). The first translation into Italian was made by Bramante's pupil, Cesare Cesariano (Como, 1521), a facsimile of which was published in 1968. The 1521 edition was soon plagiarised by Lutio (Venice, 1524) and Caporali (Perugia, 1536); but they were all superseded by Daniele Barbaro's edition (Venice, 1556 and later), which has woodcut illustrations by Palladio (see plate 163). The standard modern editions of Vitruvius are those by M. Morgan (Harvard 1914, and later paperbacks) and F. Granger (Loeb ed., London 1934).

Alberti's *De re aedificatoria* was obviously modelled on Vitruvius, even to its division into ten Books. During Alberti's lifetime it circulated only in MS, but it was printed at Florence as early as 1485 – probably, therefore, just before the first printed edition of Vitruvius. There are Italian translations by P. Lauro (Venice, 1546) and the more important one by Cosimo Bartoli (Florence, 1550 and Venice, 1565), which was also the first to be illustrated. This was translated into English by the Venetian architect Giacomo Leoni (London, 1726 and later) and has been re-issued by J. Rykwert (London, 1955). The *De re aedificatoria* has been reprinted in the original Latin with an Italian translation and notes by G. Orlandi (Milan, 2 vols., 1966).

Two other, less important, treatises were written in the fifteenth century and circulated in MS. Filarete's *Trattato di Architettura*, written before 1464, is a curious combination of a fairy-tale about a lost ancient city and a description of an ideal city, built according to classical rules, which Filarete desired to see realized by a modern ruler. An edition (New Haven/London, 1965) by J. Spencer provides a facsimile of the MS in Florence, originally presented by the author to Piero de' Medici, and a complete English translation (see pp. 107–9). An Italian edition edited by A. Finoli and L. Grassi was published in two volumes in Milan in 1972. Francesco di Giorgio also wrote a treatise on architecture, versions of which are datable 1456/1502, one of which was known to Leonardo da Vinci. A version was published in Turin in 1841, but the modern edition by Maltese and Maltese Degrassi was published in Milan in 1967.

The extraordinary *Hypnerotomachia Poliphili* – best described as an architectural novelette – is hardly a treatise, but its importance was very great. It was first printed by Aldus Manutius at Venice in 1499, and is arguably one of the most beautiful books ever produced. A splendid facsimile was published in London in 1963.

A short account has already been given (pp. 195ff) of Serlio's treatise: for a complete bibliographical account see W.B. Dinsmoor in *Art Bulletin*, XXIV, 1942. To this should be added the publication in facsimile of the 1619 edition (London, 1964) as well as the previously unpublished MS of Book VI (Milan, 2 vols., 1966) and the MS in the Avery Library, New York, in facsimile (New York, 1978). Vignola's *Regola delli Cinque Ordini d'Architettura* was published in 1562 (probably in Rome). From the seventeenth century onwards there have been many French and English translations (Vignola was particularly influential in France), but there is no mod·rn edition. The original MS is in the Uffizi, Florence.

Palladio's great work is the *Quattro Libri dell'Architettura* first published in Venice in 1570 (facsimile edition, Milan 1945 and later), and many times reprinted. It was the foundation of English and American Palladianism, and there are English translations of 1676, 1683, and 1733 (all by G. Richards), but the important ones are those by G. Leoni (London, 1715–20, and 1742, with notes from Inigo Jones's copy), Colen Campbell (Book I only, 1729) and I. Ware (London, 1738; reprint New York, 1965). Palladio's other works include two guides to Rome, *Lantichita di Roma* (Rome, 1554) and the *Descritione de le Chiese, Statione . . . in la Citta de Roma* (also Rome 1554), both of which have been republished in facsimile in P. Murray, *Five Early Guides to Rome and Florence* (Farnborough, 1972). Barbaro's Vitruvius edition had illustrations by Palladio, who also published an edition of Caesar's *Commentaries*, with illustrations, in 1575. His drawings of Roman antiquities (see pl. 160) were probably made with a view to publication: Lord Burlington published them in 1730 (reprinted 1969). The drawings are now among the treasures of the Royal Institute of British Architects in London. Palladio's successor, Vincenzo Scamozzi, also published *Discorsi sopra l'antichità di Roma* (Venice, 1582) as well as his better-known, long, and very pedestrian *Dell'Idea dell'Architettura universale* (Venice, 1615), English editions of which appeared in 1669 and many later editions. A facsimile of the 1615 edition was published in London, in two volumes, in 1964.

The catalogue of *The Fowler Architectural Collection of The Johns Hopkins University*, by L. Fowler and E. Baer (Baltimore, 1961), is a splendid work of bibliographical reference for these and many other architectural treatises.

Apart from the treatises, there are several early books which are indispensable as sources of information about the architects or their works, by far the most important being Giorgio Vasari's *Vite de Piu Eccellenti Architetti, Pittori, et Scultori Italiani, da Cimabue insino a' Tempi Nostri* (Florence, 1550 and 1568). The standard edition is still that of G. Milanesi, in 9 vols., (Florence, 1878–85, reprinted in paperback, 1973), but there is now a convenient, up-to-date edition published originally by the Club del Libro (Milan, 1962–6) in 8 vols. The great modern edition by R. Bettarini and P. Barocchi, which reprints the text of both the 1550 and the 1568 editions, is in progress (Florence, 1966–   ). There are several English translations, all based on the 1568 text, both complete and in selections. The best complete text is still that of G. de Vere in 10 vols, (London, 1912–15), but this unfortunately was never provided with notes. It has recently been reprinted in facsimile. The most useful selection is that published in the Penguin Classics series, in a new translation by George Bull (1965 and later). The *Life of Brunelleschi*, now generally attributed to Manetti, has recently appeared in a modern edition by D. De Robertis and G. Tanturli (Milan, 1976); the English edition by H. Saalman and C. Enggass (Pennsylvania and London, 1970) was made from earlier editions of the very difficult Tuscan text. Short selections from these and other writers can be found in E.G. Holt, *A Documentary History of Art*, vols. 1 and 2, New York, 1957–8, and also in D. Chambers, *Patrons and Artists in the Italian Renaissance* (London, 1970), which contains some documents dealing with architecture. *Scritti Rinascimentali di Architettura*, ed. A. Bruschi and others (Milan, 1978), contains a selection of original texts, with notes.

Much information about buildings, especially altered ones, can be gained from old engravings (which are usually beautiful in themselves), and the most important of these are the sets issued in the sixteenth and seventeenth centuries by Dupérac, Lafreri, Ferrerio and others, some of which have been reproduced here. Ferrerio and Falda's *Palazzi di Roma* of 1655 has been reprinted in facsimile, 1967. These engravings were often made up in sets to suit the customer, so that it is impossible to be certain that a given building will be in every set: the greatest to be issued as a standard set was undoubtedly the *Edifices de Rome moderne* by P. Letarouilly (3 vols. 1840–57). This has been reprinted in a selection (London, 1944 and later), and Letarouilly's other great undertaking, incomplete at his death, dealing with St Peter's and the Vatican (1863 and 1882) has also been reprinted in 2 vols., 1953–63.

2 The historians

The study of Italian architecture should start from an acquaintance with Italian life, art, and history. Jacob Burckhardt's *Civilization of the Renaissance in Italy*, first published in 1860, has been reprinted in English many times and is still essential reading. A more modern treatment is D. Hay, *The Italian Renaissance in its Historical Background* (1961 and later).

For the general principles of classical architecture I know of no better introduction than Sir John Summerson's *Classical Language of Architecture* (1963 and later; revised edition 1980). Geoffrey Scott's *Architecture of Humanism*, first published in 1914, is now dated but is still an admirable exposition of the qualities sought by an architect working within the classical tradition. Another point of view will be found in the even older *Renaissance and Baroque* by Heinrich Wölfflin (1888: English translation 1964) but the standard modern book is R. Wittkower's *Architectural Principles in the Age of Humanism* (3rd. ed. 1962), by far the most significant work on the subject. N. Pevsner's *Outline of European Architecture* (particularly the Jubilee ed., 1960) contains an important chapter on Italian architecture, and should in any case be read as an introduction to architectural history. The celebrated *History* by Bannister Fletcher (18th ed. 1975) contains an enormous number of plans, sections and other drawings often not easily available elsewhere, as well as a glossary of technical terms, but it is not altogether satisfactory as a history. The technical terminology of architecture is often a stumbling-block, although in fact the few really necessary terms are soon learned.

Since the first edition of this book was published two invaluable guides have appeared: the *Penguin Dictionary of Architecture*, by J. Fleming, H. Honour and N. Pevsner (1966 and later), which contains short biographies of all the major architects as well as definitions, in some cases illustrated, of technical terms; and J. Harris and J. Lever, *Illustrated Glossary of Architecture, 850–1830* (1966). This is unlike earlier glossaries in that it is very fully illustrated, so that the reader does not have to know in advance what word he wants to look up – by observing an unfamiliar feature in one of the buildings illustrated he is at once made aware that it is an abacus or whatever it may be.

Books dealing specifically with Italian Renaissance architecture have greatly increased in the twenty years since this one first appeared. The great Pelican History of Art now includes *Architecture in Italy, 1400–1600*, by L. Heydenreich and W. Lotz (1974); Lotz's *Studies in Italian Renaissance Architecture* also appeared in 1977, and a German classic, Burckhardt's *Architecture of the Italian Renaissance*, first published in 1867, appeared in English in 1985. Tuscany is dealt with by C. von Stegmann and H. von Geymüller in *Die Architektur der Renaissance in Toskana* (originally 11 vols., 1885–1908, abridged English version, 2 vols., New York, 1924); Venice by D. Howard, *The Architectural History of Venice* (London, 1980) and Rome in T. Magnuson's *Studies in Roman Quattrocento Architecture* (Stockholm, 1958) deals with a very restricted aspect. *The Villa in the Life of Renaissance Rome* is the title of a book by D. Coffin (1979) and the palaces of Rome have received very detailed treatment by C. Frommel in his *Römische Palastbau der Hochrenaissance* (Tübingen, 3 vols. 1973), unfortunately not available in English. Georgina Masson's *Italian Villas and Palaces* (1959), while not a history, contains many superb photographs, several of which have kindly been made available for this book. R. Goldthwaite's *Building of Renaissance Florence* (1980) is an economic and social history but vitally relevant to architecture.

The *Encyclopedia of World Art* (15 vols., 1959–69) contains many biographical and general articles, uneven in quality and length, but all with very full bibliographies. For biographical details the new *Macmillan Encyclopedia of Architects* (4 vols., New York 1982) has the most up-to-date information, again with bibliographies.

Some monographs on individual architects are followed by a few books of great importance on more general themes, not all of them in English.

ALBERTI: J. Gadol (1969), F. Borsi (1977). BRAMANTE: A. Bruschi (1977), based on a much larger monograph in Italian (Bari and Rome, 1969). BRUNELLESCHI: E. Battisti (1981), and H. Saalman (1980) on the dome of Florence Cathedral, part of a forthcoming monograph. GIULIO ROMANO: F. Hartt (1958), E. Verheyen, *The Palazzo del Tè* (1977). LEONARDO: J.P. Richter, *The Literary Works of Leonardo* (1970) for Leonardo's architectural MSS; C. Pedretti, *A Chronology of Leonardo da Vinci's Architectural Studies after 1500* (1962). MICHELANGELO: J. Ackerman (1961 and revised paperback ed. 1970). PALLADIO: J. Ackerman (1966), L. Puppi (1975), and H. Burns and others, Catalogue of the Palladio Exhibition (London, 1975). A complete corpus of Palladio's works (9 vols. so far) has been in progress since 1968 (English ed.

published by Pennsylvania State University). O. Bertotti-Scamozzi's *Fabbriche . . . di Palladio* (1796) has been reprinted with an introduction by J.Q. Hughes (1968). SANMICHELI: E. Langęnskiöld (Uppsala, 1938, but in English). SANSOVINO: D. Howard (1975).

Although not in English, the following must be mentioned as large-scale works on the churches of Rome and Florence: W. and E. Paatz, *Die Kirchen von Florenz*, 6 vols., 1940–54; W. Buchowiecki, *Handbuch der Kirchen Roms*, 3 vols., 1967–74, and the series *Roma Cristiana*, ed. C. Galassi-Paluzzi, especially vol. IV, *Le Chiese di Roma dall' XI al XVI Secolo*, by V. Golzio and G. Zander (1963).

ACKNOWLEDGMENTS

The writing of this book has incurred many obligations, and I hope that this expression of my gratitude will be some return for all the help I have received. Above all, Dr Margaret Whinney and Sir Anthony Blunt taught me most of what I know. The Photographic Department at the Courtauld Institute, and especially Dr Peter Kidson and Miss Ursula Pariser, have been (as always) kind, and have often made me photographs at what I well know was far too short notice. Mr John Gage and Mr Leslie Parris helped me in many ways. Mr Samuel Carr improved the manuscript by some skilful editing, but there would have been no manuscript at all without the indispensable and constant help of Mrs E. T. Walton.

For the generosity with which they allowed me to use their material I should like to thank Professor James Ackerman, Professor and Mrs W. Paatz, the Library of the Royal Institute of British Architects, and Professor Rudolf Wittkower.

List of Illustrations

65 Leonardo da Vinci, architectural drawing
c. 1489 or later. Paris, Institut de France:
MS 'B'. From J. P. Richter, *The Literary
Works of Leonardo da Vinci*, Oxford University Press

66 Milan, Sta Maria presso S. Satiro
Plan. 1470s. From F. Cassina, *Le Fabbriche
più cospicue di Milano*

67 Milan, Sta Maria presso S. Satiro
Section. From F. Cassina, *Le Fabbriche più
cospicue di Milano*

68 Milan, Sta Maria presso S. Satiro
Interior. 1470s. Photo: Argozzini

69 Milan, Sta Maria presso S. Satiro
Exterior. Photo: Alinari

70 Milan, Sta Maria delle Grazie
Plan. Late 1480s and 1490s. From A. Pica,
*Il Gruppo Monumentale di Sta Maria delle
Grazie*

71 Milan, Sta Maria delle Grazie
Section. From A. Pica, *Il Gruppo Monumentale di Sta Maria delle Grazie*

72 Milan, Sta Maria delle Grazie
Interior. Photo: Argozzini

73 Milan, S. Ambrogio, the Doric Cloister
1490s. Photo: P. J. Murray

74 Rome, Sta Maria della Pace
Cloister. Completed 1504. Photo: Anderson

75 Rome, S. Pietro in Montorio, Tempietto
1502. From A. Palladio, *I Quattro Libri
dell'Architettura*

76 Rome, S. Pietro in Montorio, Tempietto
Exterior. 1502. Photo: Linda Murray

77 Rome, S. Pietro in Montorio, Tempietto
Plan. From S. Serlio, *Architettura*

78 Rome, House of Raphael
c. 1512. From an engraving by A. Lafrerin.
Photo: Oscar Savio

79 Rome, House of Raphael
Palladio drawing. Royal Institute of British
Architects, London

80 Rome, Vatican
Belvedere Court. Reconstruction by Professor Ackerman. From J. Ackerman, *The
Cortile del Belvedere*

81 Rome, Vatican
Belvedere Court. Elevation. Early 16th century. From S. Serlio, *Architettura*

82 Rome, St Peter's
Caradosso's Foundation Medal, 1506.
London, British Museum

83 Rome, St Peter's
Bramante's plan. Florence, Uffizi. Photo:
Florence, Soprintendenza alle Gallerie

84 Rome, St Peter's
Menicantonio de' Chiarellis' drawing. Collection of Mr Paul Mellon

85 Montepulciano, S. Biagio
Plan and section. 1518–45. From W. Anderson and J. Stratton, *The Architecture of the
Renaissance in Italy*

86 Montepulciano, S. Biagio
Interior. Photo: Linda Murray

87 Montepulciano, S. Biagio
Exterior. Photo: Linda Murray

88 Rome, St Peter's
Bramante's dome. From S. Serlio, *Architettura*

89 Rome, St Peter's
Bramante's first plan. From W. Anderson
and J. Stratton, *The Architecture of the Renaissance in Italy*

90 Rome, St Peter's
Antonio da Sangallo the Younger's model.
Rome, Museo Petriano. Photo: Mansell-Anderson

91 Rome, St Peter's
Michelangelo's plan. Engraving by E.
Dupérac

92 Rome, St Peter's
Exterior. Engraving by E. Dupérac

93 Rome, St Peter's
Plan as built. From W. Anderson and J.
Stratton, *The Architecture of the Renaissance in
Italy*

94 Rome, S. Eligio degli Orefici
Interior of dome. Photo: Linda Murray

95 Rome, Palazzo Vidoni-Caffarelli
Exterior. Engraving. From P. Ferrerio,
Palazzi di Roma

96 Rome, Palazzo Branconio dell'Aquila. c.
1520
Engraving. From P. Ferrerio, *Palazzi di Roma*

97 Rome, Palazzo Spada
Exterior. Mid-16th century. Photo: Georgina
Masson

98 Florence, Palazzo Pandolfini
Exterior. Early 16th century. Photo: Alinari

99 Rome, Villa Madama
Exterior. Begun c. 1516. Photo: Anderson

100 Rome, Villa Madama
The loggia. Photo: Georgina Masson

101 Rome, Villa Madama
Plan. From W. E. Greenwood, *The Villa Madama, Rome*, Alec Tiranti Limited

102 Mantua, Pallazo del Tè
Plan. *c.* 1526–34. From G. Paccagnini, *Il Palazzo Tè*, Cassa di Risparmio, Mantua

103 Mantua, Palazzo del Tè
Exterior. Photo: Anderson

104 Mantua, Palazzo del Tè
Doorway. Photo: P. J. Murray

105 Mantua, Palazzo del Tè
Court. Photo: Edwin Smith

106 Mantua, Palazzo del Tè
Garden front. Photo: Edwin Smith

107 Mantua, Palazzo del Tè
Atrium. Photo: Edwin Smith

108 Mantua, Palazzo Ducale
Courtyard 'della Mostra'. Photo: Georgina Masson

109 Mantua, Giulio Romano's house
Exterior. 1540s. Photo: Alinari

110 Rome, Villa Farnesina. 1509–11
Exterior. Engraving. From P. Ferrerio, *Palazzi di Roma*

111 Rome, Villa Farnesina
Plan. From P. Letarouilly, *Edifices de Rome Moderne*

112 Rome, Villa Farnesina
Sala delle Prospettive. Photo: Gabinetto Fotografico Nazionale

113 Rome, Palazzo Massimi alle Colonne
Plan. Begun 1532/35. From P. Letarouilly, *Edifices de Rome Moderne*

114 Rome, Palazzo Massimi alle Colonne
Exterior. Photo: Anderson

115 Rome, Palazzo Massimi alle Colonne
Court. Photo: Anderson

116 Rome, Palazzo Farnese
Plan. Begun, enlarged 1534–46. From P. Letarouilly, *Edifices de Rome Moderne*

117 Rome, Palazzo Farnese
Entrance. From P. Letarouilly, *Edifices de Rome Moderne*

118 Rome, Palazzo Farnese
Exterior. Photo: Alinari

119 Rome, Palazzo Farnese
Reconstruction of Sangallo the Younger's design. From P. Letarouilly, *Edifices de Rome Moderne*

120 Rome, Palazzo Farnese
Court. Photo: Anderson

121 Florence, wooden model for façade of S. Lorenzo
Florence, Casa Buonarroti. Photo: Alinari

122 Florence, S. Lorenzo, Medici Chapel
Interior. Photo: Mansell-Brogi

123 Florence, S. Lorenzo, Medici Chapel
Section. 1520s. From C. von Stegmann and H. von Geymüller, *The Architecture of the Renaissance in Tuscany*

124 Florence, S. Lorenzo, Medici Chapel
Michelangelo's monument to Giuliano de' Medici. Photo: Alinari

125 Florence, Biblioteca Laurenziana
Vestibule. Begun 1524. Photo: Mansell-Alinari

126 Florence, Biblioteca Laurenziaña
Vestibule staircase. Photo: Alinari

127 Rome, Capìtol
Michelangelo's plan. Begun 1546. Engraving by E. Dupérac

128 Rome, Capitol
Michelangelo's design. Engraving by E. Dupérac. Photo: Oscar Savio

129 Rome, Capitol, Palazzo Capitolino
Façade. From P. Letarouilly, *Edifices de Rome Moderne*

130 Rome, Capitol, Palazzo Capitolino
Exterior, detail. Photo: Alinari

131 Rome, Porta Pia
Begun 1562. Engraving by E. Dupérac. Photo: Oscar Savio

132 Verona, Porta Palio
1530s. Photo: Alinari

133 Verona, Palazzo Pompei
Exterior. Begun *c.* 1530. Photo: Georgina Masson

134 Verona, Palazzo Canossa
Plan. Làte 1530s. From Francesco Zanotto, *Le fabbriche civili, ecclesiastiche e militari di M. San Micheli disegnate ed incise da F. Ronzani e G. Luciotti,* 1875(?)

135 Verona, Palazzo Canossa
Exterior. Photo: Georgina Masson

136 Verona, Palazzo Bevilacqua
Exterior. Designed before 1537. Photo: Georgina Masson

247

Index